No Tears Spanish Grammar

Easy Learning: Essential Rules for Beginners

Olivia Bennett

Contents

1

Welcome to Spanish Grammar!

Embarking on the adventure of learning Spanish is like opening a door to a vibrant, richly diverse world. From the sun-drenched streets of Seville to the bustling markets of Mexico City, and the captivating landscapes of Patagonia to the rhythmic beats of Havana, Spanish serves as a bridge to myriad cultures, histories, and stories. This book, "Welcome to Spanish Grammar," is your compass and map, designed to guide you through the beautiful intricacies of Spanish grammar, making the journey not just informative but also rewarding.

Our Approach

This book is crafted with the beginner in mind, breaking down the seemingly daunting aspects of Spanish grammar into digestible, manageable pieces. We believe in a holistic approach, combining the rules of grammar with the vibrant culture and real-life usage that brings the language to life. Each chapter unfolds a new aspect of grammar, woven together with practical examples, cultural insights, and tips that cater to both your logical understanding and intuitive feel for the language.

What You'll Discover

- The Spanish Sound: Learn the alphabet, understand vowels and consonants, master accentuation, and practice with diphthongs to perfect your pronunciation.

- Nouns & Articles: Explore gender and number agreements, dive into the use of definite and indefinite articles, and grasp gender and number agreement tips.

- Verbs: Gain a solid understanding of regular and irregular verbs, including present tense conjugations, stem changes, and special forms for making negative sentences and asking questions.

- Question Formation: Master the art of crafting questions, from basic structures to using interrogative words, and navigating yes/no and tag questions.

- Prepositions: Navigate through common prepositions, their use for expressing locations and time, and how they integrate with verbs.

- Adjectives and Adverbs: Delve into the use of descriptive adjectives, learn about placement, types, making comparisons, and incorporating adverbs of frequency for richer expression.

- Tackling Tenses: Traverse the landscape of Spanish tenses, from present basics to the nuances of the subjunctive mood, understanding when and how to use each.

- Pronouns Perfected: Master personal, demonstrative, and possessive pronouns, and learn the principles of pronoun placement to enhance clarity in your sentences.

Achieving Fluency

Fluency is not a destination but a journey. By the end of this book, you'll have a solid foundation in Spanish grammar, enabling you to form sentences, engage in basic conversations, and understand written and spoken Spanish. You'll have the tools to continue expanding your vocabulary, refining your pronunciation, and delving deeper into complex grammatical structures. Most importantly, you'll have the confidence to practice, make mistakes, learn from them, and keep improving.

The Path Ahead

As you turn each page, remember that every great journey begins with a single step. Your dedication, curiosity, and passion for learning Spanish are what will propel you forward. Embrace the challenges, celebrate your milestones, and immerse yourself in the rich tapestry of Spanish language and culture.

"Welcome to Spanish Grammar" is your companion on a journey of discovery, connection, and growth. So take a deep breath, open the first chapter, and let's embark on this exciting adventure together. Bienvenidos al maravilloso mundo del español (Welcome to the wonderful world of Spanish)!

2

The Spanish Sound

The Alphabet

The Spanish alphabet is your fundamental toolkit for starting your journey in learning Spanish. It consists of 27 letters, which includes all the letters from the English alphabet plus one extra character, the "ñ." This unique letter represents a sound not found in English, showing the distinctiveness of the Spanish language right from the start.

Learning the Spanish alphabet is crucial because it lays the groundwork for pronunciation, spelling, and reading. Each letter has its own name and sound, some of which are similar to their English counterparts, while others are quite different. For example, the letter "j" is pronounced like an English "h" as in "house," and "v" sounds much like "b" in Spanish, which can be confusing for beginners.

Starting with the basics, focus on familiarizing yourself with each letter's pronunciation. This will not only help you read and write in Spanish but also improve your pronunciation of words. Practice saying the letters out loud, and use Spanish alphabet songs or drills available online to help memorize them. Mastery of the Spanish alphabet is the first step towards building a strong foundation in the language.

A - ah (like 'a' in "father")

B - beh (similar to 'b' in "bed"; can sound like 'v' in some dialects)

C - ceh (before 'e' or 'i', sounds like 's' in "cent" in Latin America and like 'th' in "think" in Spain; before 'a', 'o', 'u', sounds like 'k' in "cat")

D - deh (similar to 'd' in "dog", but softer between vowels)

E - eh (like 'e' in "bed")

F - efe (like 'f' in "fine")

G - heh (before 'e' or 'i', sounds like a harsh 'h'; before 'a', 'o', 'u', sounds like 'g' in "go")

H - ah-che (silent, not pronounced)

I - ee (like 'ee' in "see")

J - hota (like 'h' in "hat", but harsher)

K - ka (like 'k' in "kite")

L - ele (like 'l' in "love")

M - eme (like 'm' in "mother")

N - ene (like 'n' in "nose")

Ñ - eñe (like 'ny' in "canyon")

O - oh (like 'o' in "sole", but more pure)

P - peh (like 'p' in "pat")

Q - cu (always followed by 'u'; pronounced like 'k' in "quake")

R - ere (a single tap of the tongue against the roof of the mouth, similar to the 'tt' in "butter" in American English; a rolling sound when doubled or at the beginning of words)

S - ese (like 's' in "snake")

T - teh (like 't' in "top", but with the tongue closer to the teeth)

U - oo (like 'oo' in "food")

V - uve (similar to 'b' in "bed"; can sound like 'v' in some dialects)

W - doble uve/doble ve (only used in foreign words, pronounced like 'w' in "water")

X - equis (like 'ks' in "kicks"; in some words, can sound like 's' or 'h')

Y - i griega (like 'y' in "yes" in most cases; can sound like 'ee' in "see" when used as a vowel)

Z - zeta (like 's' in "snake" in Latin America; like 'th' in "thin" in Spain)

While the modern Spanish alphabet comprises 27 letters, there are notable digraphs—combinations of two letters to represent a single sound—that are essential for pronunciation but are not considered separate letters. These include 'll' and 'ch.' 'Ll' represents a sound that varies regionally, often pronounced similar to the 'y' in 'yes' in many dialects. 'Ch,' on the other hand, represents a sound similar to the English 'ch' in 'church.' Both digraphs play a crucial role in distinguishing word meanings and are key to mastering Spanish pronunciation.

Remember, the pronunciation can vary significantly between different Spanish-speaking regions, especially for letters like "c", "ll", and "y". Listening to native speakers from various countries will help you get accustomed to these differences.

Vowels: The Soul of Spanish Sounds

Vowels are essential in Spanish, as they influence the pronunciation and meaning of words significantly. Spanish vowels are straightforward, consisting of five sounds: a, e, i, o, u. Each vowel has a clear, distinct sound, which is consistent regardless of the word, making them easier to learn than English vowels, which can vary widely.

- A is pronounced as in "father," a deep, open sound.

- E takes on the sound similar to the "e" in "bed," but it's a bit clearer.

- I is pronounced like the "ee" in "see," sharp and long.

- O is as in "sole," but without the diphthong sound common in English, making it more pure.

- U sounds like "oo" in "food," again, a clear and stable sound.

Vowels form the backbone of Spanish pronunciation, as they are present in every word and often determine the word's stress and rhythm. Incorrect vowel sounds can lead to misunderstandings or mispronunciations, so it's important to get them right from the start.

One effective way to practice is by repeating words that contain each vowel, paying close attention to your mouth and tongue placement. Listening to native Spanish speakers and mimicking their pronunciation can also be incredibly helpful. Remember, Spanish vowels are never silent and always play a crucial role in the language's melody and expression.

Consonants

Consonants in Spanish give the language its rhythm and flow. While some Spanish consonants have sounds similar to their English counterparts, others are quite unique, creating the distinct melody of Spanish speech. Understanding these differences is key to mastering Spanish pronunciation.

- B/V: Both 'b' and 'v' share the same sound in Spanish, a soft, buzzing sound similar to the 'b' in "ball". The lips slightly touch, making it less forceful than the English 'v'.

- C: The 'c' has two sounds. Before 'a', 'o', 'u', it's hard like the 'k' in "cat". Before 'e', 'i', it softens to a 's' sound in Latin America, like in "cent", or a 'th' sound in Spain, as in "think".

- D: Spanish 'd' is softer than in English. Between vowels, it's almost a gentle 'th', like in "this".

- G: Like 'c', 'g' changes based on the following letter. Before 'e', 'i', it's a harsh 'h' sound. Elsewhere, it's a hard 'g' as in "go". After 'n', as in "cognate", it softens further, verging on the sound of 'w' in "wow".

- H: Always silent, the 'h' is the ghost of Spanish words. It makes its presence known only in spelling, not in sound.

- J: This letter is pronounced with a strong, aspirated 'h' sound, much like the 'h' in "hot" but with more force.

- LL: Once distinct, 'll' often sounds like the 'y' in "yes" today. However, in some regions, it retains a unique sound, closer to the 'j' in "jeopardy".

- Ñ: Unique to Spanish, 'ñ' is pronounced like 'ny' in "canyon", giving Spanish its characteristic sound in words like "niño" (child).

- R: A single 'r' is lightly tapped, similar to the 'tt' in "butter" (in American English). A double 'rr' rolls off the tongue, a trill that is quintessentially Spanish.

- Z: In Latin America, 'z' is pronounced like the 's' in "snake". In Spain, it takes on a 'th' sound, as in "thin".

Mastering Spanish consonants involves listening closely to native speakers and practicing regularly. Try mimicking the sounds in words and sentences to get the hang of these unique characteristics.

Accentuation

Accentuation, or the stress of a word, is a fundamental aspect of Spanish pronunciation that can change the meaning of words. Understanding Spanish accent rules will help you correctly pronounce words and understand spoken Spanish better.

- Stress Rules: In Spanish, words are generally stressed on the penultimate (second-to-last) syllable if they end in a vowel, 'n', or 's'. If they end in any other consonant, the stress falls on the last syllable. Exceptions are marked with an accent (á, é, í, ó, ú), which indicates that the stressed syllable is not where it would normally be.

- Accented Vowels: When a vowel carries an accent mark, it not only indicates the syllable that should be stressed but can also change the word's meaning. For example, "el" (the) vs. "él" (he).

- Diphthongs and Triphthongs: In combinations of two or three vowels, stress can affect how these vowels are pronounced together. Generally, the stress falls on the strong vowel (a, e, o) in the combination.

- Special Cases: Words that break the usual stress rules will have an accent mark. This helps distinguish between words that are spelled the same but have different meanings and pronunciations, like "sí" (yes) and "si" (if).

Learning to recognize and apply Spanish accentuation rules is essential for proper pronunciation and understanding. It's a matter of paying attention to the rhythm of the language and practicing speaking and listening with the stress patterns in mind. Over time, this aspect of Spanish grammar will become second nature, enhancing both your speaking and listening skills in Spanish.

Dipping into Diphthongs

Diphthongs in Spanish are fascinating because they involve the combination of two vowels in the same syllable, creating a unique sound that flows smoothly from one vowel to the next.

A diphthong occurs when a strong vowel (a, e, o) pairs up with a weak vowel (i, u), or when two weak vowels come together. The beauty of diphthongs is in their blend; they glide together in a single syllable. For example, in the word "tierra" (earth), the 'ie' forms a diphthong, and in "ciudad" (city), the 'ua' does the same.

Here are some key combinations to listen for and practice:

- ai/au as in "aire" (air) and "pausa" (pause), where the sound starts at the strong vowel and glides into the weak one.

- ei/eu found in "reina" (queen) and "neutro" (neutral), blending seamlessly from one vowel to the next.

- oi/ou as in "oigo" (I hear) and "pou" (a colloquial expression), which mix the open sounds with a swift move to the weak vowel.

- ia/ie/io/iu showcased in words like "familia" (family), "tierra", "radio" (radio), and "viudo" (widower), demonstrating the versatility of the 'i' in diphthongs.

- ua/ue/uo/ui as in "agua" (water), "cuerpo" (body), "cuota" (quota), and "fuimos" (we went), where 'u' takes the lead in the glide.

Practicing these sounds will help you master the rhythm and melody of Spanish. Each diphthong adds color and character to your speech, allowing for a more authentic pronunciation.

3

Nouns & Articles in Action

Introduction to Spanish Nouns

Nouns are the building blocks of language, naming everything around us from places and people to ideas and feelings. In Spanish, nouns play a crucial role not just in vocabulary but also in the structure and flow of sentences. Understanding nouns is your first step into the vibrant world of Spanish language, unlocking the ability to talk about a wide array of subjects.

In Spanish, nouns are categorized into two types: common nouns (nombres comunes) and proper nouns (nombres propios). Common nouns refer to general items, such as "libro" (book), "ciudad" (city), and "amor" (love). They capture the essence of everyday things we discuss, think about, and interact with. Proper nouns, on the other hand, are used to name specific entities. These include names of people ("María", "Carlos"), places ("México", "Barcelona"), and even particular days or months ("martes", "julio"). Proper nouns are always capitalized in Spanish, just like in English, marking them as distinct and significant.

Understanding the difference between common and proper nouns helps you navigate the basics of Spanish grammar and usage. It sets the stage for deeper learning about how nouns interact with other words in sentences, particularly verbs and adjectives. Furthermore, grasping the concept of nouns allows you to start forming simple sentences, describing the world around you in Spanish with increasing confidence and clarity.

The Gender of Nouns

One of the unique features of Spanish, compared to English, is that all nouns have a gender. They are either masculine or feminine, which influences how sentences are structured, especially when it comes to articles and adjectives. This concept may seem daunting at first, but with some practice and a few tips, it becomes second nature.

Masculine nouns often end in "-o", such as "amigo" (friend) and "libro" (book), while feminine nouns frequently end in "-a", like "amiga" (friend) and "casa" (house). This rule is a good starting point for guessing the gender of nouns. However, there are exceptions. For instance, "mano" (hand) is feminine despite ending in "-o". Similarly, "día" (day) is masculine even though it ends with "-a".

There are also nouns that end in other letters, which can follow different patterns. Nouns ending in "-ción" or "-sión", like "nación" (nation) and "televisión" (television), are typically feminine. Meanwhile, nouns ending in "-ma", such as "problema" (problem) and "sistema" (system), are often masculine, borrowed from Greek where they were masculine as well.

Here are some tips for remembering noun genders:

- Associate the noun with a specific article in your study or flashcards: "el" for masculine nouns and "la" for feminine nouns. For example, learning "el libro" and "la casa" instead of just "libro" and "casa".

- Look for patterns in word endings as mentioned above, but be mindful of exceptions by making a special note of them.

- Practice with sentences and contexts, not just isolated words. Using nouns in phrases helps solidify their gender in your memory due to the agreement with other words.

Remember, while many nouns follow the general "-o" for masculine and "-a" for feminine rule, the exceptions make Spanish a rich and intriguing language. Encountering and learning these exceptions will enhance your vocabulary and understanding of Spanish grammar, adding depth to your conversations and writing. Keep practicing, and soon, identifying the gender of Spanish nouns will become an intuitive part of your language skills.

Exercises on The Gender of Nouns

Exercise 1: Identifying Gender

Choose the correct article ("el" for masculine, "la" for feminine) for each noun.

___ amigo

___ casa

___ mano

___ problema

Exercise 2: Masculine or Feminine?

Indicate whether the noun is masculine (M) or feminine (F).

lección ( )

mapa ( )

agua ( )

niño ( )

Answers

Exercise 1:

el amigo - "Amigo" ends in "-o", which typically indicates a masculine noun.

la casa - "Casa" ends in "-a", commonly marking feminine nouns.

la mano - Despite ending in "-o", "mano" is an exception and is feminine.

el problema - "Problema" ends in "-ma" and is masculine, following the pattern of Greek-origin nouns.

Exercise 2:

lección (F) - Nouns ending in "-ción" are usually feminine.

mapa (M) - "Mapa" is an exception to the typical rule, being masculine.

agua (F) - Although it starts with "a-", "agua" is feminine but uses "el" in the singular form to avoid the double "a" sound (el agua).

niño (M) - Ends in "-o", indicating it is masculine.

Number Agreement

In Spanish, like in English, nouns can be singular or plural. However, forming plurals in Spanish follows specific rules that are slightly different from English. Understanding these rules is essential for correct sentence construction and for making sure your words agree in number as well as in gender.

The basic rule for forming plurals is simple: if a noun ends in a vowel, add "-s"; if it ends in a consonant, add "-es". For example, "libro" (book) becomes "libros" (books), and "ciudad" (city) turns into "ciudades" (cities). This pattern helps maintain the rhythm and harmony of Spanish pronunciation.

There are a few exceptions to these rules:

- Nouns ending in "-z" change the "z" to "c" before adding "-es" to form the plural. For instance, "luz" (light) becomes "luces" (lights).

- If a noun ends in a vowel with an accent (á, é, í, ó, ú), you still add "-s", but keep an eye on those accents since they might affect pronunciation. For example, "sofá" becomes "sofás".

- Some nouns have irregular plural forms or remain unchanged in the plural, especially if they're borrowed from other languages.

Plural formation in Spanish also extends to articles and adjectives, which must agree in number and gender with the nouns they modify. This agreement is crucial for the clarity and correctness of your speech and writing.

Exercises on Number Agreement

Exercise 1: Forming Plurals

Convert the following singular nouns to their plural forms.

chico (boy)

mujer (woman)

lápiz (pencil)

ley (law)

análisis (analysis)

Exercise 2: Matching Plurals with Articles

Match the plural noun with its correct plural article.

amigos (A. las, B. los)

casas (A. los, B. las)

universidades (A. los, B. las)

relojes (A. los, B. las)

Exercise 3: Plural Adjectives Agreement

Make the adjective agree in number with the given plural noun.

niño feliz (happy boy) → niños __

ciudad grande (big city) → ciudades __

Answers

Exercise 1:

chico → chicos - Add "-s" because it ends in a vowel.

mujer → mujeres - Add "-es" because it ends in a consonant.

lápiz → lápices - Change "-z" to "-c" and add "-es".

ley → leyes - Add "-es" because it ends in a consonant.

análisis → análisis - Remains unchanged in plural, as it's an exception.

Exercise 2:

amigos (B. los) - "Amigos" is masculine plural, so it matches with "los".

casas (B. las) - "Casas" is feminine plural, matching with "las".

universidades (B. las) - "Universidades" is feminine plural, so it uses "las".

relojes (A. los) - "Relojes" is masculine plural, despite the ending, and matches with "los".

Exercise 3:

niños felices - Adjective "feliz" changes to "felices" to agree with masculine plural noun "niños".

ciudades grandes - Adjective "grande" changes to "grandes" to match the feminine plural noun "ciudades".

Definite Articles

Definite articles in Spanish, much like "the" in English, are used to refer to specific nouns. However, Spanish takes it a step further by varying the article based on the gender and number of the noun it precedes. There are four definite articles: "el" (masculine singular), "la" (feminine singular), "los" (masculine plural), and "las" (feminine plural).

Using the correct definite article is crucial for clear communication in Spanish. Here's how to match them with noun gender and number:

- Use "el" for singular masculine nouns, like "el libro" (the book).

- Use "la" for singular feminine nouns, such as "la casa" (the house).

- For plural masculine nouns, switch to "los", like "los libros" (the books).

- For plural feminine nouns, use "las", as in "las casas" (the houses).

Remember, the article must always agree with the noun in both gender and number. This agreement is a fundamental aspect of Spanish grammar, helping to indicate the specificity and detail of conversation or text.

As you advance in your Spanish learning journey, paying attention to these details becomes second nature, allowing you to communicate more precisely and fluently.

Exercises on Definite Articles

Exercise 1: Choosing the Correct Definite Article

Choose the correct definite article for each noun.

___ sol (sun)

___ ventana (window)

___ amigos (friends)

___ flores (flowers)

Exercise 2: Matching Nouns with Definite Articles

Match the noun with its correct definite article.

perro (A. la, B. el)

mesas (A. los, B. las)

reloj (A. las, B. el)

estrellas (A. los, B. las)

Answers

Exercise 1:

el sol - "Sol" is masculine singular, so it uses "el".

la ventana - "Ventana" is feminine singular, hence "la".

los amigos - "Amigos" is masculine plural, requiring "los".

las flores - "Flores" is feminine plural, so "las" is correct.

Exercise 2:

perro (B. el) - "Perro" is masculine singular, matching with "el".

mesas (B. las) - "Mesas" is feminine plural, so it pairs with "las".

reloj (B. el) - "Reloj" is masculine singular, thus "el" is the correct choice.

estrellas (B. las) - "Estrellas" is feminine plural, correctly matched with "las".

Indefinite Articles

While definite articles in Spanish point to something specific, indefinite articles are used to refer to nonspecific items or quantities. They're the equivalent of "a," "an," and "some" in English, and just like their definite counterparts, they change form based on the gender and number of the noun they accompany. The four indefinite articles in Spanish are "un" (masculine singular), "una" (feminine singular), "unos" (masculine plural), and "unas" (feminine plural).

- Un is used before masculine singular nouns that start with a consonant sound, for example, "un libro" (a book).

- Una is for feminine singular nouns, like "una casa" (a house).

- Unos and unas are used to indicate some or a few of something in the plural form, such as "unos libros" (some books) and "unas casas" (some houses).

The choice between "un" and "una" can sometimes be straightforward, aligning with the natural gender of the noun. However, remembering the correct article becomes trickier with nouns whose gender isn't immediately apparent. Here, memorization and practice come into play.

Indefinite articles are essential in conversation and writing when you're referring to an unspecified quantity of something or introducing a new topic that hasn't been mentioned before. They set the stage for descriptions, comparisons, and general statements about people, places, and things.

Exercises on Indefinite Articles

Exercise 1: Selecting the Correct Indefinite Article

Choose the correct indefinite article for each noun.

___ amigo (friend)

___ ciudad (city)

___ libros (books)

___ flores (flowers)

Exercise 2: Fill in the Blanks with Indefinite Articles

Fill in the blanks with "un," "una," "unos," or "unas" as appropriate.

Tengo ___ gato en mi casa. (I have a cat in my house.)

Vimos ___ estrellas en el cielo. (We saw some stars in the sky.)

Hay ___ manzana en la mesa. (There is an apple on the table.)

Compré ___ revistas ayer. (I bought some magazines yesterday.)

Answers

Exercise 1:

un amigo - "Amigo" is masculine singular, so "un" is used.

una ciudad - "Ciudad" is feminine singular, hence "una".

unos libros - "Libros" is masculine plural, requiring "unos".

unas flores - "Flores" is feminine plural, so "unas" is correct.

Exercise 2:

Tengo un gato en mi casa. - "Gato" is masculine singular, so "un" is appropriate.

Vimos unas estrellas en el cielo. - "Estrellas" is feminine plural, thus "unas" is used.

Hay una manzana en la mesa. - "Manzana" is feminine singular, making "una" the correct choice.

Compré unas revistas ayer. - "Revistas" is feminine plural, so "unas" fits.

Gender and Number Agreement Tips

Mastering gender and number agreement in Spanish can seem daunting at first, but with a few strategies and practice, it becomes much easier. Here are some tips to help you navigate the complexities of noun gender and ensure your sentences are grammatically harmonious:

- Look for Patterns: While there are exceptions, many nouns follow common gender patterns (e.g., nouns ending in "-o" are often masculine, and those ending in "-a" are usually feminine). Familiarizing yourself with these patterns can help you guess the gender of new nouns you encounter.

- Use Mnemonics: Create mnemonic devices to remember exceptions to the rules. For instance, "la mano" (the hand) is feminine despite ending in "-o". Associating "mano" with another feminine word or concept can help it stick in your memory.

- Practice with Sentence Construction: Regularly constructing sentences with new vocabulary can reinforce the correct gender and number agreement. Writing and speaking exercises allow you to apply the rules in context, making it easier to remember them.

- Learn Nouns with Their Articles: When you learn a new noun, memorize it along with its definite or indefinite article ("el" or "un" for masculine nouns and "la" or "una" for feminine nouns). This helps cement the noun's gender in your memory.

- Listen and Repeat: Listening to native speakers and repeating after them can also help you internalize gender and number agreements. Pay attention to how articles, nouns, and adjectives are used in sentences to get a feel for natural Spanish grammar.

By incorporating these strategies into your study routine, you'll find that gender and number agreements become more intuitive over time, allowing you to communicate in Spanish more confidently and accurately.

4

The Verb: Regular Verbs

Introduction to Spanish Verbs

Verbs are the action words in a sentence, telling us what the subject is doing. In Spanish, verbs are the heartbeat of communication, bringing life and movement to the language. They're a bit like chameleons, changing form to match the subject they're connected to, as well as the time frame of the action. Understanding how verbs work in Spanish is crucial for expressing yourself accurately and fluently.

At their core, Spanish verbs are based on infinitives. Infinitives are the base form of the verb, the way they appear in the dictionary, before any changes are made to match the subject or tense. In English, infinitives are preceded by "to," as in "to eat" or "to live." In Spanish, infinitives end in one of three ways: -ar (like "hablar", to talk), -er (like "comer", to eat), or -ir (like "vivir", to live). These endings tell you how the verb changes or conjugates.

Conjugation is the process of altering a verb to indicate who is doing the action and when it's happening. Spanish conjugation might seem daunting because it's more complex than in English. Every subject (I, you, he, she, we, they) requires a different verb form in each tense. But don't worry! Once you learn the patterns, it starts to make a lot of sense.

The verb infinitive endings (-ar, -er, -ir) are the key to unlocking these patterns. They determine how verbs are conjugated in different tenses, starting with the present tense, which is the focus of our next discussion. By mastering verb conjugations, you open up a world of communication possibilities, allowing you to share your thoughts, actions, and feelings with others in Spanish.

Present Tense: -AR Verbs

Conjugating -ar verbs in the present tense is your first step into the vibrant world of Spanish action words. The present tense is used to talk about habits, routines, facts, and actions happening right now. Let's dive into how to transform an -ar verb from its infinitive form to match each subject.

The process is straightforward once you grasp the pattern. Here's a step-by-step guide using "hablar" (to talk) as our example:

- Start with the infinitive: hablar

- Remove the infinitive ending (-ar): habl-

- Add the present tense endings:

- Yo hablo (I talk)

- Tú hablas (You talk, informal)

- Él/Ella/Usted habla (He/She/You formal talks)

- Nosotros/Nosotras hablamos (We talk)

- Vosotros/Vosotras habláis (You all talk, informal, used mainly in Spain)

- Ellos/Ellas/Ustedes hablan (They/You all formal talk)

By following these steps, you can conjugate any regular -ar verb in the present tense. Remember, the key to learning verb conjugations is practice and repetition. The more you use these verbs in sentences, the more natural it will feel. Start by making simple sentences with each conjugated form. For example, "Yo estudio español" (I study Spanish) or "Ellos caminan al parque" (They walk to the park). With regular practice, conjugating -ar verbs in the present tense will become second nature, enhancing your ability to communicate effectively in Spanish.

Exercises on Present Tense: -AR Verbs

Exercise 1: Conjugate the Verb

Conjugate the verb "estudiar" (to study) in the present tense for each subject.

Yo (I)

Tú (You, informal)

Él/Ella/Usted (He/She/You formal)

Nosotros/Nosotras (We)

Vosotros/Vosotras (You all, informal, Spain)

Ellos/Ellas/Ustedes (They/You all formal)

Exercise 2: Fill in the Blanks

Complete the sentences with the correct form of "caminar" (to walk).

Yo ___ al colegio todos los días. (I walk to school every day.)

Nosotros ___ en el parque. (We walk in the park.)

Ella ___ con su perro por la mañana. (She walks with her dog in the morning.)

Exercise 3: Choose the Correct Conjugation

Select the correct form of "cantar" (to sing) for each sentence.

Tú ___ en la ducha. (a) cantas (b) canto (c) cantamos

Ellos ___ en el coro. (a) canta (b) cantáis (c) cantan

Vosotros ___ muy bien. (a) canta (b) cantáis (c) cantan

Answers

Exercise 1:

Yo estudio (I study)

Tú estudias (You study, informal)

Él/Ella/Usted estudia (He/She/You formal studies)

Nosotros/Nosotras estudiamos (We study)

Vosotros/Vosotras estudiáis (You all study, informal, Spain)

Ellos/Ellas/Ustedes estudian (They/You all formal study)

The endings -o, -as, -a, -amos, -áis, and -an are added to the stem "estudi-" to match each subject pronoun.

Exercise 2:

Yo camino al colegio todos los días.

Nosotros caminamos en el parque.

Ella camina con su perro por la mañana.

"Camino," "caminamos," and "camina" are the correct conjugations of "caminar" for "yo," "nosotros/nosotras," and "ella," respectively, following the pattern for regular -ar verbs.

Exercise 3:

Tú (a) cantas en la ducha.

Ellos (c) cantan en el coro.

Vosotros (b) cantáis muy bien.

The correct options match the subject pronoun with the appropriate ending for regular -ar verbs in the present tense. "Cantas" for "tú," "cantan" for "ellos/ellas/ustedes," and "cantáis" for "vosotros/vosotras."

Present Tense: -ER Verbs

Diving into -er verbs, we find ourselves exploring another vibrant group of Spanish verbs. These verbs, which include actions like "comer" (to eat) and "aprender" (to learn), follow a specific pattern in the present tense that's as systematic as it is for -ar verbs, yet with its own set of endings.

To conjugate regular -er verbs in the present tense, you'll follow a similar process to -ar verbs but with a twist in the endings. Here's how it unfolds:

- Begin with the infinitive: For example, "comer."

- Remove the -er ending: This leaves you with "com-."

- Add the present tense -er endings:

- Yo como (I eat)

- Tú comes (You eat, informal)

- Él/Ella/Usted come (He/She/You formal eats)

- Nosotros/Nosotras comemos (We eat)

27

- Vosotros/Vosotras coméis (You all eat, informal, mainly in Spain)

- Ellos/Ellas/Ustedes comen (They/You all formal eat)

These endings are what differentiate -er verbs from -ar verbs, giving them their unique conjugation pattern in the present tense.

Let's apply this pattern with "aprender" (to learn):

- Yo aprendo

- Tú aprendes

- Él/Ella/Usted aprende

- Nosotros/Nosotras aprendemos

- Vosotros/Vosotras aprendéis

- Ellos/Ellas/Ustedes aprenden

Exercises on Present Tense: -ER Verbs

Exercise 1: Conjugate the Verb

Conjugate the verb "beber" (to drink) in the present tense for each subject.

Yo (I)

Tú (You, informal)

Él/Ella/Usted (He/She/You formal)

Nosotros/Nosotras (We)

Vosotros/Vosotras (You all, informal, Spain)

Ellos/Ellas/Ustedes (They/You all formal)

Exercise 2: Fill in the Blanks

Complete the sentences with the correct form of "leer" (to read).

Yo __ revistas de ciencia. (I read science magazines.)

Nosotros __ en la biblioteca a menudo. (We read in the library often.)

Ellos __ el periódico todos los días. (They read the newspaper every day.)

Exercise 3: Choose the Correct Conjugation

Select the correct form of "vender" (to sell) for each sentence.

Tú __ productos orgánicos. (a) vendo (b) vendes (c) venden

Usted __ en el mercado. (a) vende (b) vendes (c) vendemos

Nosotras __ nuestra ropa vieja. (a) vendéis (b) venden (c) vendemos

Answers

Exercise 1:

Yo bebo (I drink)

Tú bebes (You drink, informal)

Él/Ella/Usted bebe (He/She/You formal drinks)

Nosotros/Nosotras bebemos (We drink)

Vosotros/Vosotras bebéis (You all drink, informal, Spain)

Ellos/Ellas/Ustedes beben (They/You all formal drink)

The endings -o, -es, -e, -emos, -éis, and -en are added to the stem "beb-" to match each subject pronoun, following the pattern for regular -er verbs in the present tense.

Exercise 2:

Yo leo revistas de ciencia.

Nosotros leemos en la biblioteca a menudo.

Ellos leen el periódico todos los días.

"Leo," "leemos," and "leen" are the correct conjugations of "leer" for "yo," "nosotros/nosotras," and "ellos/ellas/ustedes," respectively. This showcases the application of -er verb endings in sentences.

Exercise 3:

Tú (b) vendes productos orgánicos.

Usted (a) vende en el mercado.

Nosotras (c) vendemos nuestra ropa vieja.

The correct options are chosen based on the subject pronoun and the regular -er verb conjugation pattern. "Vendes" matches "tú," "vende" aligns with "usted," and "vendemos" fits "nosotras," illustrating how the verb endings change to agree with the subject in number and person.

Present Tense: -IR Verbs

-IR verbs round out our exploration of regular verb conjugations in Spanish. This group includes verbs like "vivir" (to live) and "escribir" (to write), offering a fresh set of endings to master for the present tense.

Conjugating -ir verbs follows a process similar to -ar and -er verbs, but with its own unique endings:

- Start with the infinitive: For instance, "vivir."

- Remove the -ir ending: Leaving "viv-."

- Add the present tense -ir endings:

- Yo vivo (I live)

- Tú vives (You live, informal)

- Él/Ella/Usted vive (He/She/You formal lives)

- Nosotros/Nosotras vivimos (We live)

- Vosotros/Vosotras vivís (You all live, informal, mainly in Spain)

- Ellos/Ellas/Ustedes viven (They/You all formal live)

These endings highlight the distinct pattern for -ir verbs, marking them apart from their -ar and -er cousins.

By mastering the conjugation of -ar, -er, and -ir verbs in the present tense, you unlock the ability to express a wide array of actions and states of being in Spanish. Regular practice with these verbs, across all their forms, will greatly enhance your comfort and fluency in everyday Spanish conversation.

Exercises on Present Tense: -IR Verbs

Exercise 1: Conjugate the Verb

Conjugate the verb "abrir" (to open) in the present tense for each subject.

Yo (I)

Tú (You, informal)

Él/Ella/Usted (He/She/You formal)

Nosotros/Nosotras (We)

Vosotros/Vosotras (You all, informal, Spain)

Ellos/Ellas/Ustedes (They/You all formal)

Exercise 2: Fill in the Blanks

Complete the sentences with the correct form of "escribir" (to write).

Yo ___ una carta a mi amigo. (I write a letter to my friend.)

Ustedes ___ correos electrónicos. (You all write emails.)

Ella ___ en su diario cada noche. (She writes in her diary every night.)

Exercise 3: Choose the Correct Conjugation

Select the correct form of "decidir" (to decide) for each sentence.

Nosotros ___ ir al cine esta noche. (a) decides (b) decidís (c) decidimos

Tú ___ qué comer. (a) decido (b) decides (c) deciden

Vosotras ___ sobre el proyecto. (a) decide (b) decidís (c) deciden

Answers

Exercise 1:

Yo abro (I open)

Tú abres (You open, informal)

Él/Ella/Usted abre (He/She/You formal opens)

Nosotros/Nosotras abrimos (We open)

Vosotros/Vosotras abrís (You all open, informal, Spain)

Ellos/Ellas/Ustedes abren (They/You all formal open)

"Abrir" is conjugated according to the -ir verb endings in the present tense, which are -o, -es, -e, -imos, -ís, and -en for each respective subject pronoun.

Exercise 2:

Yo escribo una carta a mi amigo.

Ustedes escriben correos electrónicos.

Ella escribe en su diario cada noche.

These sentences demonstrate the use of "escribir" conjugated in the first person singular (yo), second person plural formal (ustedes), and third person singular (ella) in the present tense.

Exercise 3:

Nosotros (c) decidimos ir al cine esta noche.

Tú (b) decides qué comer.

Vosotras (b) decidís sobre el proyecto.

The correct options reflect the conjugation of "decidir" in the present tense for "nosotros" (we decide), "tú" (you decide, informal), and "vosotras" (you all decide, informal, Spain). The endings -imos, -es, and -ís are correctly matched with each subject pronoun, showcasing the unique -ir verb endings in the present tense.

Forming Negative Sentences

Turning a sentence from affirmative to negative in Spanish is surprisingly straightforward. The key player here is the word "no," which acts as the gatekeeper to negativity. Unlike English, where negation can require additional auxiliary verbs or rearranging words, Spanish keeps it simple: place "no" directly before the verb.

Let's break it down with an example. The affirmative sentence "Tú comes manzanas" (You eat apples) becomes negative by adding "no" before the verb: "Tú no comes manzanas" (You do not eat apples).

This rule holds true across all regular verbs and subjects:

- Yo hablo (I speak) becomes Yo no hablo (I do not speak).

- Nosotros vivimos aquí (We live here) turns into Nosotros no vivimos aquí (We do not live here).

For sentences with auxiliary verbs or phrases like "quiero" (I want) or "puedo" (I can), "no" precedes the auxiliary: "Yo no quiero comer" (I do not want to eat), "Ella no puede venir" (She cannot come).

Exercises on Forming Negative Sentences

Exercise 1: Turn into Negative

Convert the following affirmative sentences into negative sentences.

Ellos estudian español.

Yo quiero ir al cine.

Nosotros podemos jugar fútbol.

Exercise 2: Choose the Correct Negative Sentence

Select the correct negative form of each sentence.

Tú bailas salsa.

a) Tú no baila salsa.

b) Tú no bailas salsa.

Ella tiene un libro.

a) Ella no tiene un libro.

b) Ella no tiene libro.

Ustedes ven la televisión.

a) Ustedes no ven la televisión.

b) Ustedes ven no la televisión.

Answers

Exercise 1:

Ellos estudian español. → Ellos no estudian español.

"No" is placed directly before the verb "estudian" to negate the sentence.

Yo quiero ir al cine. → Yo no quiero ir al cine.

"No" precedes the auxiliary verb "quiero" to form the negative.

Nosotros podemos jugar fútbol. → Nosotros no podemos jugar fútbol.

The negative is formed by adding "no" before "podemos," the auxiliary verb.

Exercise 2:

b) Tú no bailas salsa.

Correct placement of "no" before the verb "bailas" follows the rule for negation.

a) Ella no tiene un libro.

"No" directly before the verb "tiene" correctly negates the sentence.

a) Ustedes no ven la televisión.

Option a) correctly places "no" before the verb "ven" to negate the sentence.

Adverbs of Frequency

Adverbs of frequency are the secret spice of language that help you express how often something happens. In Spanish, just like in English, these adverbs can dramatically change the meaning of a sentence by indicating the frequency of an action. Some common adverbs of frequency include "siempre" (always), "nunca" (never), "a menudo" (often), "a veces" (sometimes), and "raramente" (rarely).

The placement of these adverbs in a sentence is quite flexible, but they are commonly positioned either before the main verb or between an auxiliary verb and the main verb. For instance, you might say, "Yo siempre estudio después de clases" (I always study after class) or "Ellos nunca comen carne" (They never eat meat).

Here's how adverbs of frequency can modify the meaning of regular verbs in the present tense:

- "Siempre" (Always): Implies that the action is done without fail, as in "Ella siempre llega temprano" (She always arrives early).

- "Nunca" (Never): Indicates that the action is not done at any time, e.g., "Yo nunca olvido tu cumpleaños" (I never forget your birthday).

- "A menudo" (Often): Suggests a high frequency, but not constant, as in "Nosotros comemos pescado a menudo" (We often eat fish).

- "A veces" (Sometimes): Used for actions that occur occasionally, "Tú a veces trabajas desde casa" (You sometimes work from home).

- "Raramente" (Rarely): Implies the action is infrequent, "Ellos raramente ven televisión" (They rarely watch TV).

Understanding and using adverbs of frequency will allow you to add nuance to your conversations in Spanish. It lets you share not just what you do, but how often you do it, giving others a deeper insight into your habits, routines, and preferences.

Exercises on Adverbs of Frequency

Exercise 1: Match the Adverb to Its Meaning

Match each Spanish adverb of frequency with its English equivalent.

Siempre ( )

Nunca ( )

A menudo ( )

A veces ( )

Raramente ( )

a. Always

b. Never

c. Often

d. Sometimes

e. Rarely

Exercise 2: Insert the Adverb

Choose the most appropriate adverb of frequency from the list to complete each sentence. (Siempre, Nunca, A menudo, A veces, Raramente)

Yo __ voy al gimnasio en las mañanas.

Ellos __ comen en ese restaurante.

Nosotros __ vemos películas los fines de semana.

Answers

Exercise 1:

Siempre - a. Always

Nunca - b. Never

A menudo - c. Often

A veces - d. Sometimes

Raramente - e. Rarely

Exercise 2:

Yo siempre voy al gimnasio en las mañanas. (I always go to the gym in the mornings.)

Ellos raramente comen en ese restaurante. (They rarely eat at that restaurant.)

Nosotros a veces vemos películas los fines de semana. (We sometimes watch movies on weekends.)

5

The Verb: Irregular Verbs

Introduction to Irregular Verbs

Irregular verbs in Spanish, much like their English counterparts, refuse to follow the standard rules of conjugation. While most verbs in Spanish change their endings in predictable patterns based on their infinitive endings (-ar, -er, -ir), irregular verbs do their own thing. They might change vowels in their stem, have unexpected endings, or completely transform.

But why bother with these rule-breakers? Because they're essential. Many of the most common and useful Spanish verbs are irregular. They're the verbs you use to describe who you are, what you have, where you're going, and what you're doing. Without them, it would be challenging to talk about your daily life, your needs, or even to ask simple questions.

Understanding irregular verbs is crucial for communicating effectively in Spanish. They often represent fundamental concepts and actions, so they appear frequently in both spoken and written Spanish. Mastering them means unlocking a significant part of everyday communication, allowing you to express a wide range of ideas and activities.

Common Irregular Verbs

Ser (to be)

One of the most fundamental verbs in Spanish, "ser" is used to talk about identity, characteristics, and time. Its conjugation is entirely irregular:

- Yo soy (I am)

- Tú eres (You are)

- Él/Ella/Usted es (He/She/You formal is)

- Nosotros somos (We are)

- Vosotros sois (You all are, informal, mainly in Spain)

- Ellos/Ellas/Ustedes son (They/You all formal are)

Example: "Yo soy estudiante." (I am a student.)

Tener (to have)

"Tener" is used to express possession, age, and certain conditions. It changes its stem and has an irregular yo form:

- Yo tengo (I have)

- Tú tienes (You have)

- Él/Ella/Usted tiene (He/She/You formal has)

- Nosotros tenemos (We have)

- Vosotros tenéis (You all have, informal, mainly in Spain)

- Ellos/Ellas/Ustedes tienen (They/You all formal have)

Example: "Ella tiene tres libros." (She has three books.)

Ir (to go)

"Ir" is crucial for talking about movement or plans. It's completely irregular:

- Yo voy (I go)

- Tú vas (You go)

- Él/Ella/Usted va (He/She/You formal goes)

- Nosotros vamos (We go)

- Vosotros vais (You all go, informal, mainly in Spain)

- Ellos/Ellas/Ustedes van (They/You all formal go)

Example: "Nosotros vamos al cine." (We are going to the cinema.)

Learning these verbs is like getting the keys to the city. They open up countless possibilities for expressing yourself, asking questions, and understanding others. These verbs form the backbone of Spanish communication, and while they may seem challenging at first, with practice, they'll become an integral part of your Spanish toolkit.

Exercises on Common Irregular Verbs

Exercise 1: Conjugate the Verb

Write the correct form of the verb "ser" for each subject.

Yo (I)

Tú (You, informal)

Nosotros (We)

Ellos (They)

Exercise 2: Fill in the Blanks with "Tener"

Complete the sentences with the correct form of "tener."

Yo __ dos hermanos. (I have two brothers.)

Ella __ una idea genial. (She has a great idea.)

Vosotros __ mucha prisa. (You all are in a hurry, informal, mainly in Spain.)

Answers

Exercise 1:

Yo soy (I am) - "Soy" is the first person singular form of "ser."

Tú eres (You are) - "Eres" is the second person singular form of "ser."

Nosotros somos (We are) - "Somos" is the first person plural form of "ser."

Ellos son (They are) - "Son" is the third person plural form of "ser."

This exercise helps learners practice the irregular conjugation of "ser," an essential verb for describing identity, characteristics, and time.

Exercise 2:

Yo tengo dos hermanos.

Ella tiene una idea genial.

Vosotros tenéis mucha prisa.

The correct forms of "tener" (to have) are used based on the subject pronoun, demonstrating the verb's irregular stem change and conjugation in the present tense.

Stem-Changing Verbs: e > ie

Stem-changing verbs in Spanish are like magical shape-shifters of the language, changing their inner vowel when conjugated, except in the *nosotros* and *vosotros* forms. The *e > ie* transformation is one of the most common types of stem changes. It might seem like a tiny tweak, but it's powerful enough to alter the pronunciation and keep the language's rhythm intact.

Take "pensar," meaning "to think." In its stem, the *e* changes to *ie* in most of its present tense forms:

- Yo pienso (I think)

- Tú piensas (You think)

- Él/Ella/Usted piensa (He/She/You formal thinks)

- Nosotros pensamos (We think)

- Vosotros pensáis (You all think, informal, mainly in Spain)

- Ellos/Ellas/Ustedes piensan (They/You all formal think)

Notice the *e* to *ie* change doesn't apply to *nosotros* and *vosotros* forms. This pattern is a guidepost for navigating *e > ie* stem-changing verbs.

Another verb undergoing this transformation is "cerrar" (to close):

- Yo cierro (I close)

- Tú cierras (You close)

- Él/Ella/Usted cierra (He/She/You formal closes)

- Nosotros cerramos (We close)

- Vosotros cerráis (You all close, informal, mainly in Spain)

- Ellos/Ellas/Ustedes cierran (They/You all formal close)

Exercises on Stem-Changing Verbs: e > ie

Exercise 1: Conjugate the Verb

Conjugate the verb "empezar" (to start) in the present tense for each subject.

Yo (I)

Tú (You, informal)

Él/Ella/Usted (He/She/You formal)

Nosotros (We)

Ellos (They)

Exercise 2: Fill in the Blanks with the Correct Form

Complete the sentences with the correct form of "entender" (to understand).

Yo no ___ bien el español. (I do not understand Spanish well.)

¿___ tú las instrucciones? (Do you understand the instructions?)

Ellos siempre ___ todo en clase. (They always understand everything in class.)

Answers

Exercise 1:

Yo empiezo (I start) - "Empiezo" follows the e > ie stem change.

Tú empiezas (You start) - "Empiezas" includes the stem change.

Él/Ella/Usted empieza (He/She/You formal starts) - "Empieza" shows the e > ie change.

Nosotros empezamos (We start) - "Empezamos" does not undergo the stem change.

Ellos empiezan (They start) - "Empiezan" includes the stem change.

"Empezar" demonstrates the e > ie stem change in the present tense, except for "nosotros," where the original stem is preserved.

Exercise 2:

Yo no entiendo bien el español.

¿Entiendes tú las instrucciones?

Ellos siempre entienden todo en clase.

"Entender" changes from e > ie in the present tense, except in the "nosotros" form. This exercise practices applying the stem change to convey understanding in different contexts.

Stem-Changing Verbs: o > ue

The *o > ue* stem change is another enchanting aspect of Spanish verbs, showcasing the language's tendency to keep you on your toes. This change occurs in the same way as *e > ie*, affecting all forms except *nosotros* and *vosotros*.

Consider "poder," which means "to be able to" or "can." Its conjugation showcases the *o > ue* shift:

- Yo puedo (I can)

- Tú puedes (You can)

- Él/Ella/Usted puede (He/She/You formal can)

- Nosotros podemos (We can)

- Vosotros podéis (You all can, informal, mainly in Spain)

- Ellos/Ellas/Ustedes pueden (They/You all formal can)

Another example is "dormir" (to sleep), which also follows this pattern:

- Yo duermo (I sleep)

- Tú duermes (You sleep)

- Él/Ella/Usted duerme (He/She/You formal sleeps)

- Nosotros dormimos (We sleep)

- Vosotros dormís (You all sleep, informal, mainly in Spain)

- Ellos/Ellas/Ustedes duermen (They/You all formal sleep)

Exercises on Stem-Changing Verbs: o > ue

Exercise 1: Conjugate the Verb

Conjugate the verb "volver" (to return) in the present tense for each subject.

Yo (I)

Tú (You, informal)

Él/Ella/Usted (He/She/You formal)

Nosotros (We)

Ellos (They)

Exercise 2: Fill in the Blanks with the Correct Form

Complete the sentences with the correct form of "encontrar" (to find).

Yo __ mis llaves en el sofá. (I find my keys on the sofa.)

Ellos __ un perro en la calle. (They find a dog on the street.)

Nosotras __ interesante la película. (We find the movie interesting.)

Answers

Exercise 1:

Yo vuelvo (I return) - "Vuelvo" shows the o > ue stem change.

Tú vuelves (You return) - "Vuelves" includes the stem change.

Él/Ella/Usted vuelve (He/She/You formal returns) - "Vuelve" demonstrates the o > ue change.

Nosotros volvemos (We return) - "Volvemos" does not undergo the stem change, following the rule for "nosotros" and "vosotros."

Ellos vuelven (They return) - "Vuelven" includes the stem change.

"Volver" is conjugated with the o > ue stem change in all present tense forms except for "nosotros" and "vosotros," illustrating the pattern for stem-changing verbs.

Exercise 2:

Yo encuentro mis llaves en el sofá.

Ellos encuentran un perro en la calle.

Nosotras encontramos interesante la película.

"Encontrar" follows the o > ue stem change except in "nosotros/nosotras" form. This exercise helps practice recognizing and applying the stem change in different contexts.

Stem-Changing Verbs: e > i

The *e > i* stem change in Spanish verbs is yet another twist in the tapestry of verb conjugations, providing a layer of depth and nuance to the language. This change occurs within the verb stem in the present tense for all forms except, once again, *nosotros* and *vosotros*. It's fascinating how these small changes can significantly affect the pronunciation and meaning of verbs, making them essential for effective communication.

Understanding e > i Changes

In verbs like "pedir" (to ask for) and "servir" (to serve), the *e* in the stem changes to *i* in the present tense:

- Pedir:

  - Yo pido (I ask for)

  - Tú pides (You ask for)

  - Él/Ella/Usted pide (He/She/You formal asks for)

  - Nosotros pedimos (We ask for)

  - Vosotros pedís (You all ask for, informal, mainly in Spain)

  - Ellos/Ellas/Ustedes piden (They/You all formal ask for)

- Servir:

  - Yo sirvo (I serve)

  - Tú sirves (You serve)

  - Él/Ella/Usted sirve (He/She/You formal serves)

  - Nosotros servimos (We serve)

o Vosotros servís (You all serve, informal, mainly in Spain)

o Ellos/Ellas/Ustedes sirven (They/You all formal serve)

Exercises on Stem-Changing Verbs: e > i

Exercise 1: Conjugate the Verb

Conjugate the verb "repetir" (to repeat) in the present tense for each subject.

Yo (I)

Tú (You, informal)

Él/Ella/Usted (He/She/You formal)

Nosotros (We)

Ellos (They)

Exercise 2: Fill in the Blanks with the Correct Form

Complete the sentences with the correct form of "seguir" (to follow, to continue).

Yo __ las instrucciones cuidadosamente. (I follow the instructions carefully.)

Nosotras __ estudiando para el examen. (We continue studying for the exam.)

Ellos __ sin parar. (They continue without stopping.)

Answers

Exercise 1:

Yo repito (I repeat) - Demonstrates the e > i stem change.

Tú repites (You repeat) - Includes the stem change.

Él/Ella/Usted repite (He/She/You formal repeats) - Shows the e > i change.

Nosotros repetimos (We repeat) - Does not undergo the stem change, following the rule for "nosotros" and "vosotros."

Ellos repiten (They repeat) - Includes the stem change.

"Repetir" follows the e > i stem change in the present tense, except in the "nosotros" and "vosotros" forms, illustrating the pattern for e > i stem-changing verbs.

Exercise 2:

Yo sigo las instrucciones cuidadosamente.

Nosotras seguimos estudiando para el examen.

Ellos siguen sin parar.

"Seguir" changes from e > i in the present tense, except in the "nosotros/nosotras" form, which remains as "seguimos." This exercise helps practice applying the stem change in sentences that describe continuing actions.

Irregular Yo Forms

Some Spanish verbs throw a curveball by being regular in most of their forms but irregular in the first person singular (*yo*) present tense. This peculiarity adds a layer of complexity and richness to the language, showcasing its diversity and flexibility.

Exploring Irregular Yo Forms

These verbs might follow the regular patterns for all forms except for the *yo* form, where they decide to stand out. Examples include:

- Salir (to go out):

  - Yo salgo

  - Tú sales

  - Él/Ella/Usted sale

  - Nosotros salimos

  - Vosotros salís

  - Ellos/Ellas/Ustedes salen

- Hacer (to do/make):

  - Yo hago

  - Tú haces

  - Él/Ella/Usted hace

  - Nosotros hacemos

  - Vosotros hacéis

  - Ellos/Ellas/Ustedes hacen

- Traer (to bring):

  - Yo traigo

  - Tú traes

  - Él/Ella/Usted trae

  - Nosotros traemos

  - Vosotros traéis

- Ellos/Ellas/Ustedes traen

Understanding the Irregularities

The irregular *yo* forms often result from historical phonetic changes or the language's evolution, providing insight into Spanish's dynamic nature. While these irregularities may seem daunting at first, they are part of the common verbs you'll use frequently, making them important to learn early on.

Exercises on Irregular Yo Forms

Exercise 1: Identify the Correct Yo Form

Choose the correct "yo" form of each verb.

Salir

a) salo

b) salgo

c) sale

Hacer

a) haco

b) hago

c) hace

Traer

a) traigo

b) traer

c) traes

Exercise 2: Conjugate in Sentences

Fill in the blanks with the correct "yo" form of the verb in parentheses.

Yo __ tarde al trabajo hoy. (llegar)

Yo __ una tarta para la fiesta. (hacer)

Yo __ con mis amigos después de clase. (encontrar)

Answers

Exercise 1:

b) salgo - The correct "yo" form of "salir" is "salgo" (I go out).

b) hago - The correct "yo" form of "hacer" is "hago" (I do/make).

a) traigo - The correct "yo" form of "traer" is "traigo" (I bring).

These irregular "yo" forms are the result of historical linguistic changes and are exceptions to the regular conjugation patterns.

Exercise 2:

Yo llego tarde al trabajo hoy. - "Llego" is the regular "yo" form of "llegar" (to arrive), not irregular but used for context.

Yo hago una tarta para la fiesta. - "Hago" is the irregular "yo" form of "hacer" (to make).

Yo encuentro con mis amigos después de clase. - "Encuentro" follows the stem-changing pattern (e > ie) for "encontrar" (to meet), not an irregular "yo" form but used for practicing verb conjugation in context.

6

Asking Questions in Spanish

The Basics of Forming Questions

Asking questions is a fundamental aspect of learning any language, and Spanish is no exception. The beauty of forming questions in Spanish lies in its simplicity and flexibility. Two main methods are commonly used: intonation and inversion.

Intonation: Much like in English, you can ask a question in Spanish by simply raising the pitch of your voice at the end of a statement. This method doesn't require rearranging the sentence structure. For example, the statement "Tú hablas español" (You speak Spanish) can become a question with just a change in tone: "¿Tú hablas español?" (Do you speak Spanish?).

Inversion: Another way to form questions is by inverting the order of the subject and the verb. While this is more common in English, it's less frequently used in Spanish but still perfectly valid. For instance, "Tú hablas español" can be inverted to "¿Hablas tú español?" Although this structure is understood, it's more common to see it without inversion, relying on intonation and question marks in writing.

Here are some basic question structures with regular verbs:

- AR Verbs: "¿Estudias tú español?" (Do you study Spanish?)

  - Without inversion: "¿Tú estudias español?"

- ER Verbs: "¿Comes tú verduras?" (Do you eat vegetables?)

  - Without inversion: "¿Tú comes verduras?"

- IR Verbs: "¿Vives tú en esta ciudad?" (Do you live in this city?)

  - Without inversion: "¿Tú vives en esta ciudad?"

These examples highlight the straightforward nature of crafting questions in Spanish. The key is understanding the role of intonation and punctuation, especially the use of the inverted question mark (¿) at the beginning of written questions, a unique feature of Spanish.

Exercises on The Basics of Forming Questions

Exercise 1: Change Statements to Questions

Convert the following statements into questions using intonation (add question marks).

Ellos juegan al fútbol los domingos. (They play soccer on Sundays.)

Ella tiene un perro. (She has a dog.)

Nosotros vamos al cine. (We go to the cinema.)

Exercise 2: Inversion Practice

Rewrite the statements as questions by inverting the subject and verb. If inversion doesn't apply, use intonation.

Tú lees libros de aventuras. (You read adventure books.)

Ustedes estudian por la noche. (You all study at night.)

Yo escucho música clásica. (I listen to classical music.)

Answers

Exercise 1:

¿Ellos juegan al fútbol los domingos?

By adding question marks, the statement becomes a question without changing the word order.

¿Ella tiene un perro?

The same technique applies, turning the statement into a question.

¿Nosotros vamos al cine?

The statement is converted into a question through punctuation and intonation.

Exercise 2:

¿Lees tú libros de aventuras?

Inversion is used here, but keeping the original order with intonation is also correct: "¿Tú lees libros de aventuras?"

¿Estudian ustedes por la noche?

The subject and verb are inverted to form a question. Without inversion: "¿Ustedes estudian por la noche?"

¿Escucho yo música clásica?

Inversion in the first person is less common, so intonation is typically used: "¿Yo escucho música clásica?"

Interrogative Words

Diving deeper into the art of asking questions, Spanish uses a set of interrogative words that add precision and clarity. These words are essential for gathering specific information and are similar to the "wh-questions" in English. Here's a rundown of the primary interrogative words in Spanish:

- Qué (What): Used to inquire about things or information. Example: "¿Qué haces?" (What are you doing?)

- Quién (Who): For asking about people. Singular: "¿Quién viene?" (Who is coming?) and plural: "¿Quiénes son?" (Who are they?)

- Cuándo (When): To find out about time. Example: "¿Cuándo es la fiesta?" (When is the party?)

- Dónde (Where): Used to inquire about places. Example: "¿Dónde vives?" (Where do you live?)

- Por qué (Why): For understanding reasons. Example: "¿Por qué estudias español?" (Why do you study Spanish?)

- Cómo (How): To learn about manners or conditions. Example: "¿Cómo estás?" (How are you?)

The placement of these interrogative words is typically at the beginning of the question, directly influencing the sentence's structure to provide clear, specific queries.

Exercises on Interrogative Words

Exercise 1: Match the Interrogative Word to Its Use

Match each Spanish interrogative word with its correct use.

Qué ( )

Quién/Quiénes ( )

Cuándo ( )

Dónde ( )

Por qué ( )

Cómo ( )

a. Asking about reasons

b. Inquiring about time

c. Asking about manners or conditions

d. Used to inquire about things or information

e. For asking about people

f. Used to inquire about places

Exercise 2: Form Questions Using Interrogative Words

Use the provided interrogative words to form a question related to the hint.

Qué (activity)

Quién (responsibility for a task)

Dónde (location of an object)

Answers

Exercise 1:

Qué - d. Used to inquire about things or information

Quién/Quiénes - e. For asking about people

Cuándo - b. Inquiring about time

Dónde - f. Used to inquire about places

Por qué - a. Asking about reasons

Cómo - c. Asking about manners or conditions

Exercise 2:

¿Qué haces? (What are you doing?) - "Qué" is used to inquire about an activity.

¿Quién limpia la casa? (Who cleans the house?) - "Quién" is used to ask about the responsibility for a task.

¿Dónde está el libro? (Where is the book?) - "Dónde" is used to find out the location of an object.

Yes/No Questions

Forming yes/no questions in Spanish is refreshingly straightforward, offering a simplicity that encourages even the most novice learners to dive into conversations. Unlike English, which often requires auxiliary verbs ("do", "does", etc.) to form questions, Spanish gets to the point without the need for inversion or extra words.

To ask a question in Spanish that can be answered with "sí" (yes) or "no" (no), you simply raise the intonation at the end of the statement. The structure of the sentence remains unchanged. For example, the statement "Tú hablas español" (You speak Spanish) becomes a question with just a lift in your voice tone: "¿Tú hablas español?" (Do you speak Spanish?). Notice, the sentence structure didn't twist and turn; it just adopted a questioning tone and, in writing, added the opening question mark (¿).

This method's beauty lies in its efficiency and ease, empowering learners to ask questions confidently. Whether discussing favorite foods, "¿Te gusta la pizza?" (Do you like pizza?), or inquiring about someone's ability, "¿Puedes nadar?" (Can you swim?), the formula remains elegantly simple.

Exercises on Yes/No Questions

Exercise 1: Convert to Yes/No Questions

Change the following statements into yes/no questions by adjusting the intonation and adding the necessary punctuation.

Ella puede cocinar. (She can cook.)

Nosotros vamos a la playa. (We go to the beach.)

Tienes un perro. (You have a dog.)

Exercise 2: Form Your Own Yes/No Questions

Create yes/no questions using the cues provided.

(tú / vivir / en esta ciudad)

(ella / tener / hermanos)

Answers

Exercise 1:

¿Ella puede cocinar? - The statement becomes a question by simply raising the intonation at the end and adding the opening question mark, asking if she can cook.

¿Nosotros vamos a la playa? - By adjusting the tone, the sentence queries if the group is going to the beach, keeping the sentence structure intact.

¿Tienes un perro? - This transformation inquires if the person has a dog, utilizing the straightforward method of forming yes/no questions in Spanish.

Exercise 2:

¿Vives tú en esta ciudad? - Asks if you live in this city, maintaining the statement's structure while seeking a yes or no answer.

¿Ella tiene hermanos? - Inquires whether she has siblings, a straightforward yes/no question.

Tag Questions

Tag questions in Spanish, while serving a similar purpose as in English—to confirm or seek agreement—have their unique flair. The most common tag phrases are "¿verdad?" (right?) and "¿no?" (isn't it?), which can be tacked onto the end of statements to turn them into questions.

Unlike English, where the tag changes based on the statement ("isn't it?", "doesn't she?", etc.), Spanish keeps it uncomplicated with a one-size-fits-all approach. For example, "Hace frío hoy, ¿verdad?" (It's cold today, right?) or "Eres estudiante, ¿no?" (You're a student, aren't you?).

Using tag questions is an excellent way for beginners to engage in conversations, seeking affirmation or inviting others to share their perspective. It transforms statements into interactive dialogue pieces, fostering a connection between speakers.

Practice creating your tag questions. Start with a statement you're comfortable with, like "El café está caliente" (The coffee is hot), and add "¿verdad?" or "¿no?" to the end: "El café está caliente, ¿verdad?". This practice will help you become adept at gently seeking agreement or confirmation in Spanish, enhancing your conversational skills.

Exercises on Tag Questions

Exercise 1: Add a Tag Question

Convert the following statements into tag questions by adding "¿verdad?" or "¿no?" at the end.

Tú hablas inglés. (You speak English.)

La película fue interesante. (The movie was interesting.)

Ellos pueden venir mañana. (They can come tomorrow.)

Exercise 2: Choose the Correct Tag

From the options provided, select the correct way to form a tag question.

Eres profesor, __?

a) ¿verdad?

b) ¿sí?

Vamos a la playa, __?

a) ¿no?

b) ¿cómo?

Ha llovido mucho, __?

a) ¿verdad?

b) ¿por qué?

Answers

Exercise 1:

Tú hablas inglés, ¿verdad? or Tú hablas inglés, ¿no?

Adding "¿verdad?" or "¿no?" at the end turns the statement into a tag question, seeking confirmation.

La película fue interesante, ¿verdad? or La película fue interesante, ¿no?

Either tag can be used to confirm the speaker's opinion that the movie was interesting.

Ellos pueden venir mañana, ¿verdad? or Ellos pueden venir mañana, ¿no?

The tags ask for agreement or confirmation about the possibility of them coming tomorrow.

Exercise 2:

a) ¿verdad?

"¿Verdad?" is the correct tag to seek confirmation, translating to "right?" or "aren't you?" in English.

a) ¿no?

"¿No?" is used here as a tag to confirm the plan, effectively asking, "We're going to the beach, aren't we?"

a) ¿verdad?

"¿Verdad?" is the appropriate tag for seeking agreement about the statement regarding the rain, meaning "hasn't it?" in English.

Punctuation

Spanish punctuation has its own set of rules that might seem quirky at first glance, especially when it comes to asking questions. One of the most distinctive features is the use of inverted question marks (¿?). This unique punctuation mark is used at the beginning of questions, complemented by the regular question mark at the end.

Why does Spanish use this approach? The inverted question mark serves as an early signal that a question is coming up, setting the tone and mood before you even reach the end of the sentence. This is particularly helpful in longer sentences, where the questioning tone might not be clear until you've read the whole statement. For instance, "¿Vas a venir a la fiesta esta noche?" (Are you coming to the party tonight?) immediately lets the reader know a question is being asked.

Correct placement of inverted question marks is crucial in written Spanish. It helps distinguish between statements and questions, where intonation alone wouldn't suffice. Consider "Vas a la fiesta." (You are going to the party.) versus "¿Vas a la fiesta?" (Are you going to the party?). The presence of "¿?" changes the sentence from a statement to a question.

Exercises on Punctuation

Exercise 1: Add Inverted Question Marks

Insert the inverted question marks where needed to turn the statements into questions.

Vas a la escuela hoy

Ella quiere café con leche

Pueden ayudarme con esto

Exercise 2: Rewrite with Proper Punctuation

Rewrite the following sentences using both the inverted and regular question marks correctly.

Te gusta la música pop

Sabes nadar

Cuándo es tu cumpleaños

Answers

Exercise 1:

¿Vas a la escuela hoy?

¿Ella quiere café con leche?

¿Pueden ayudarme con esto?

Adding the inverted question mark at the beginning of these sentences signals to the reader that these are questions, not statements. This punctuation change is crucial for conveying the interrogative nature of the sentence in written Spanish.

Exercise 2:

¿Te gusta la música pop?

¿Sabes nadar?

¿Cuándo es tu cumpleaños?

By placing both the inverted question mark at the start and the regular question mark at the end, these sentences are correctly punctuated as questions in Spanish. This punctuation method effectively communicates the questioning tone from the beginning of the sentence, especially important for longer or complex sentences where the interrogative mood might not be immediately apparent.

Advanced Question Techniques

As you progress in your Spanish journey, you'll encounter more complex structures and verb tenses in questions. These advanced techniques allow for richer, more nuanced expressions of curiosity and hypothetical thinking.

Subjunctive and Conditional Moods: The subjunctive mood is used to express wishes, doubts, and hypothetical situations, often found in questions. For example, "¿Qué harías si ganaras la lotería?" (What would you do if you won the lottery?) uses the conditional mood ("harías", would do) and the subjunctive ("ganaras", won). The conditional mood is typically used in polite requests or to speculate about possible situations, making your questions more sophisticated.

Indirect Questions: These are questions embedded within a statement or another question, often introduced by phrases like "Quiero saber" (I want to know) or "¿Puedes decirme?" (Can you tell me?). An indirect question doesn't require an inverted question mark at the beginning and tends to follow the statement's structure. For instance, "Quiero saber dónde vives." (I want to know where you live.) Unlike direct questions, indirect questions integrate smoothly into broader statements, allowing for more complex interactions.

Strategies for Forming Advanced Questions:

- Practice transitioning between tenses within questions to match the time frame of what you're asking.

- Use subjunctive forms after phrases like "Es posible que" (It's possible that) or "Es probable que" (It's likely that) to express uncertainty or speculation.

- Incorporate conditional phrases to pose hypothetical scenarios, enhancing the depth of your inquiries.

Exercises on Advanced Question Techniques

Exercise 1: Subjunctive and Conditional Mood

Rewrite the sentences using the subjunctive or conditional mood to form a question.

What would you buy if you had a lot of money? (tener, comprar)

Where would you travel if you could fly anywhere? (poder, viajar)

Exercise 2: Indirect Questions

Convert the direct questions into indirect questions.

¿Dónde está la biblioteca? (I want to know)

¿Cuándo empieza la película? (Can you tell me)

Answers

Exercise 1:

¿Qué comprarías si tuvieras mucho dinero?

"comprarías" (would buy) uses the conditional mood to speculate about an action based on having a lot of money. "tuvieras" (had) employs the subjunctive mood to express a hypothetical situation.

¿Adónde viajarías si pudieras volar a cualquier lugar?

"viajarías" (would travel) is in the conditional mood, speculating about travel destinations. "pudieras" (could) is in the subjunctive mood, considering a hypothetical ability to fly anywhere.

Exercise 2:

Quiero saber dónde está la biblioteca.

This indirect question translates the direct question into a statement of desire to know the library's location, smoothly incorporating the inquiry.

¿Puedes decirme cuándo empieza la película?

Here, the direct question is embedded into a request for information, making it an indirect question about the movie's start time.

7

Preposition

Introduction to Prepositions

Prepositions are the unsung heroes of language, quietly working behind the scenes to connect the dots in our sentences. In Spanish, as in English, prepositions are small but mighty words that link nouns, pronouns, and phrases to other parts of a sentence, establishing relationships of time, place, direction, and more. They're the glue that holds sentences together, providing clarity and context to our conversations.

Think of prepositions as indicators or signposts, guiding us through the landscape of language. They answer questions like "Where?" (¿Dónde?), "When?" (¿Cuándo?), and "How?" (¿Cómo?), giving us the ability to describe the world around us with precision. For instance, prepositions can tell us that we are "in" a city, "on" a street, or "with" a friend.

The role of prepositions in Spanish sentences is crucial. They help to convey the relationship between the action of the verb and the noun or pronoun acting as the object of the sentence. Without prepositions, our sentences would be like puzzles with missing pieces, difficult to understand and incomplete. By mastering Spanish prepositions, you unlock the ability to express yourself more accurately and navigate conversations with greater ease.

Common Spanish Prepositions

Spanish prepositions are versatile and essential for everyday communication. Here's a closer look at some of the most common ones:

- A (to): Used to indicate direction, destination, or a specific time. It's also used in personal "a" constructions when the direct object is a person. Example: "Voy a la playa" (I'm going to the beach).

- De (of/from): Indicates possession, origin, material, and cause. It's often used to show where someone is from. Example: "Soy de México" (I'm from Mexico).

- En (in/on): Specifies location or position, and can also mean "on" in some contexts. Example: "Estoy en casa" (I'm at home).

- Con (with): Denotes accompaniment, manner, or means. Example: "Voy con mis amigos" (I'm going with my friends).

- Sin (without): Expresses absence or lack of something. Example: "Café sin azúcar" (Coffee without sugar).

Each of these prepositions plays a pivotal role in crafting meaningful and precise sentences. Let's explore them further with examples:

- A: "Asisto a clases de español" (I attend Spanish classes). Here, "a" connects the verb "asisto" with the noun phrase "clases de español," indicating the action's direction.

- De: "El libro de María" (Maria's book). "De" shows possession, linking "libro" to its owner, María.

- En: "El gato está en el tejado" (The cat is on the roof). "En" describes the cat's location.

- Con: "Hablo con el profesor" (I am speaking with the professor). "Con" indicates the company or accompaniment.

- Sin: "Salí sin mi teléfono" (I left without my phone). "Sin" tells us what the speaker is lacking.

Understanding these prepositions and their uses is key to mastering Spanish grammar. They are foundational in describing actions, locations, possessions, relationships, and much more, making your journey into Spanish a rich and rewarding experience.

Exercises on Common Spanish Prepositions

Exercise 1: Match the Preposition to Its Use

Match each preposition with its correct use from the descriptions provided.

A ( )

De ( )

En ( )

Con ( )

Sin ( )

a. Indicates possession or origin

b. Used to indicate direction or destination

c. Specifies location or position

d. Denotes accompaniment or means

e. Expresses absence or lack of something

Exercise 2: Fill in the Blanks

Choose the correct preposition to complete each sentence.

Voy __ la escuela todos los días. (to)

El regalo es __ Juan. (from)

Estamos __ el parque. (at)

Quiero café __ leche. (with)

Salgo __ mi casa sin llaves. (from/without)

Answers

Exercise 1:

A - b. Used to indicate direction or destination

De - a. Indicates possession or origin

En - c. Specifies location or position

Con - d. Denotes accompaniment or means

Sin - e. Expresses absence or lack of something

Exercise 2:

Voy a la escuela todos los días. - "A" is used to express direction ("to the school").

El regalo es de Juan. - "De" indicates origin or possession ("from Juan").

Estamos en el parque. - "En" is used for location ("at the park").

Quiero café con leche. - "Con" means "with" ("coffee with milk").

Salgo de mi casa sin llaves. - "Sin" is used for "without" ("I leave my house without keys"). Here, "de" is not used as "salir de" would imply "from," but the focus is on "without," so "sin" is correct.

Prepositions of Place

Navigating the spatial relationships in Spanish is akin to directing a play on the stage of language, where prepositions of place are the directors. These prepositions—such as "sobre" (on/over), "bajo" (under), "detrás de" (behind), and "delante de" (in front of)—set the scenes, placing characters and objects precisely where they belong.

- Sobre implies resting on the surface or being above without touching. Picture a book lying idly on a table: "El libro está sobre la mesa" (The book is on the table).

- Bajo paints a picture of something being underneath or covered by something else. Imagine a cat hiding under the bed: "El gato está bajo la cama" (The cat is under the bed).

- Detrás de signals that something is behind another, suggesting a sequence or order. Visualize standing behind a building: "Estoy detrás del edificio" (I am behind the building).

- Delante de indicates the opposite of "detrás de," placing someone or something in front of another. Think of a person standing in front of a painting: "La silla está delante del cuadro" (The chair is in front of the painting).

Exercises on Prepositions of Place

Exercise 1: Choose the Correct Preposition

Select the correct preposition of place for each sentence.

La lámpara está ___ la mesa. (on)

a) sobre

b) bajo

c) detrás de

El perro duerme ___ la cama. (under)

a) sobre

b) bajo

c) delante de

Nosotros estamos ___ la estación. (in front of)

a) sobre

b) detrás de

c) delante de

Exercise 2: Fill in the Blanks

Complete the sentences with the appropriate preposition of place.

Los zapatos están ___ el armario. (under)

El cuadro está ___ la pared. (on/over)

La planta está ___ la ventana. (in front of)

Answers

Exercise 1:

a) sobre - "La lámpara está sobre la mesa." Correct because "sobre" means "on" or "over," indicating the lamp's position on top of the table.

b) bajo - "El perro duerme bajo la cama." Correct because "bajo" means "under," indicating the dog's position beneath the bed.

c) delante de - "Nosotros estamos delante de la estación." Correct because "delante de" means "in front of," indicating the position relative to the station.

Exercise 2:

Los zapatos están bajo el armario. - "Bajo" is used to indicate that the shoes are under the closet.

El cuadro está sobre la pared. - "Sobre" indicates that the painting is on or over the wall.

La planta está delante de la ventana. - "Delante de" means the plant is located in front of the window.

Prepositions of Time

Time, with its unyielding march forward, is marked by prepositions in Spanish that help us navigate the temporal landscape. Prepositions such as "a" (at), "en" (in), "durante" (during), and "hasta" (until) serve as temporal signposts, guiding us through the when of actions and events.

- A is the pinpoint in time, the specific hour at which events occur. It sets appointments and meetings precisely on the clock: "La reunión es a las tres" (The meeting is at three).

- En offers a broader sense of time, situating events within days, months, seasons, or years: "Vamos de vacaciones en julio" (We're going on vacation in July).

- Durante stretches across the duration of an event, emphasizing the continuity of an action over time: "Leí durante el vuelo" (I read during the flight).

- Hasta marks the endpoint, the moment until which an action extends: "Trabajo hasta las cinco" (I work until five).

Exercises on Prepositions of Time

Exercise 1: Choose the Correct Preposition

Select the correct preposition of time for each sentence.

El concierto comienza ___ las ocho. (at)

a) a

b) en

c) durante

Estudiamos ___ la noche. (during)

a) a

b) en

c) durante

La tienda está cerrada ___ mayo. (in)

a) a

b) en

c) hasta

Exercise 2: Fill in the Blanks

Complete the sentences with the appropriate preposition of time.

Voy al gimnasio ___ las mañanas. (in)

La película empieza ___ las nueve. (at)

Trabajan aquí ___ junio. (until)

Answers

Exercise 1:

a) a - "El concierto comienza a las ocho." Correct because "a" is used to specify a precise time, such as the start of a concert.

c) durante - "Estudiamos durante la noche." Correct because "durante" is used to indicate an action's duration over a period, such as studying throughout the night.

b) en - "La tienda está cerrada en mayo." Correct because "en" is used to situate an event within a larger time frame, like a month.

Exercise 2:

Voy al gimnasio en las mañanas. - "En" correctly situates the action within a recurring time frame (the mornings).

La película empieza a las nueve. - "A" specifies the exact time the movie starts.

Trabajan aquí hasta junio. - "Hasta" indicates the endpoint of their work period here (until June).

Prepositions with Verbs

In Spanish, the dance between verbs and prepositions is a choreography that must be mastered for the language to flow gracefully. Certain verbs aren't complete without their prepositional partners; they're like key ingredients that make a dish come alive. For instance, "soñar con" (to dream about) and "empezar a" (to start to) are just the tip of the iceberg. Each combination creates a specific meaning that enriches your conversations and understanding.

Understanding Verb-Preposition Combinations:

- Soñar con: The preposition "con" (with) links the verb "soñar" (to dream) to the object of the dream. Example: "Sueño con viajar a España" (I dream of traveling to Spain).

- Empezar a: "Empezar" (to start) is followed by "a" to indicate the beginning of an action. Example: "Empiezo a estudiar" (I start to study).

These pairings are not random; they are fixed combinations that you'll need to memorize as single units of meaning.

Exercises on Prepositions with Verbs

Exercise 1: Match the Verb with Its Preposition

Match each verb to its corresponding preposition.

Soñar ( )

Empezar ( )

Terminar ( )

a) con

b) a

c) de

Exercise 2: Complete the Sentences

Fill in the blanks with the correct preposition based on the verb provided.

Quiero ___ aprender español. (empezar)

Ella terminó ___ leer el libro. (terminar)

Nosotros soñamos ___ ir a Japón. (soñar)

Answers

Exercise 1:

Soñar - a) con: "Soñar con" is the correct pairing, meaning "to dream about."

Empezar - b) a: "Empezar a" indicates the beginning of an action.

Terminar - c) de: While "terminar" wasn't explicitly discussed in the section, "terminar de" is a common combination meaning "to finish doing" something.

Exercise 2:

Quiero empezar a aprender español. - "a" is used with "empezar" to indicate the start of an action.

Ella terminó de leer el libro. - "de" follows "terminó" to express the completion of an action.

Nosotros soñamos con ir a Japón. - "con" is used with "soñar" to link the verb to the dream's content.

Challenging Prepositions and Common Mistakes

As you delve deeper into Spanish, you'll encounter prepositions and phrases that present a challenge due to their complexity or subtlety. Phrases like "a pesar de" (despite), "cerca de" (near), and "debajo de" (underneath) add nuance to your expressions but can be tricky to master.

Complex Prepositions:

- A pesar de: Used to express a contrast or contradiction. Example: "A pesar de la lluvia, fuimos al parque" (Despite the rain, we went to the park).

- Cerca de: Indicates proximity. Example: "Vivo cerca de la escuela" (I live near the school).

- Debajo de: Specifies something is directly under another. Example: "El gato está debajo de la mesa" (The cat is under the table).

Common Mistakes and How to Avoid Them:

- Confusing Similar Prepositions: "Por" and "para" often cause confusion due to their overlapping meanings. Remember, "por" generally implies a reason or cause, while "para" indicates purpose or destination. Practice distinguishing between them by using examples and contexts.

- Literal Translations: Directly translating prepositions from English to Spanish (and vice versa) can lead to errors, as prepositions don't always match one-to-one across languages. Focus on learning Spanish prepositions in their specific contexts.

- Overuse of 'De': While "de" is versatile, it's not a catch-all preposition. Avoid the temptation to use it as a default and learn the correct prepositions for different contexts.

- Ignoring Regional Variations: Prepositions can vary by region. Be aware of these differences, especially if you're learning a specific dialect. Exposure to diverse Spanish-speaking media can help.

To navigate these challenges, pay close attention to how native speakers use prepositions, practice regularly, and don't be afraid to make mistakes—they're valuable learning opportunities. As you become more familiar with the nuances of Spanish prepositions, you'll find yourself communicating more precisely and confidently.

Exercises on Challenging Prepositions and Common Mistakes

Exercise 1: Select the Correct Preposition

Choose the correct preposition to complete each sentence.

__ pesar de el frío, salimos a caminar. (a pesar de/cerca de/debajo de)

La biblioteca está __ de mi casa. (a pesar de/cerca de/debajo de)

Mi bolígrafo está __ de los libros. (a pesar de/cerca de/debajo de)

Exercise 2: Por vs. Para

Fill in the blanks with either "por" or "para" to correctly complete the sentences.

Estudiamos mucho __ pasar el examen.

Caminamos __ el parque todas las mañanas.

Este regalo es __ ti.

Answers

Exercise 1:

a pesar de - Correct because "a pesar de" is used to express a contrast or contradiction.

cerca de - Correct because "cerca de" indicates proximity or nearness.

debajo de - Correct because "debajo de" specifies that something is directly under another object.

Exercise 2:

para - "Estudiamos mucho para pasar el examen." Correct because "para" indicates the purpose or goal of studying.

por - "Caminamos por el parque todas las mañanas." Correct because "por" is used here to express the reason or route.

para - "Este regalo es para ti." Correct because "para" shows the intended recipient of the gift.

8

Adjective

Understanding Adjectives

In Spanish, adjectives do more than just describe; they harmonize with the nouns they modify, agreeing in gender and number, adding a layer of complexity and beauty to the language.

At their core, adjectives are words that describe or modify nouns, providing additional information about an object's size, color, shape, quality, or quantity. They answer questions like "What kind?" "How many?" and "Which one?" For example, "un libro interesante" (an interesting book) uses the adjective "interesante" to describe the noun "libro."

Spanish adjectives must agree with the nouns they describe in two key ways: gender and number. This means that if the noun is feminine and singular, the adjective must also be feminine and singular, such as "una casa blanca" (a white house), where "casa" (house) is feminine and "blanca" (white) matches it in gender and number. If the noun is masculine and plural, the adjective becomes masculine and plural as well, like "unos libros interesantes" (some interesting books).

This agreement is crucial in Spanish and differs from English, where adjectives do not change form. It's a dynamic feature that adds depth to the language, ensuring that sentences flow smoothly and coherently.

Placement of Adjectives

In English, adjectives typically precede the nouns they describe. Spanish, however, dances to a different rhythm, often placing adjectives after the nouns. This placement isn't just a grammatical rule; it shapes the meaning and emphasis of sentences, offering speakers a nuanced tool for expression.

The default position for Spanish adjectives is post-nominal, meaning they come after the noun. For instance, "un coche rápido" (a fast car) follows this pattern, with "rápido" (fast) coming after "coche" (car). This order can subtly shift the focus onto the noun, making the adjective feel like an additional, sometimes optional, detail.

However, Spanish is flexible, and certain adjectives can precede the noun, especially when they denote an inherent quality or when the speaker wishes to emphasize or express an opinion. Placing an adjective before the noun can imbue the sentence with a subjective or poetic quality, as in "viejos amigos" (old friends), suggesting a deep, established friendship rather than friends who are elderly.

The impact of placement on meaning is significant. Consider the difference between "un hombre pobre" (a poor man, in terms of wealth) and "un pobre hombre" (a poor man, suggesting pity). The adjective's position alters the sentence's nuance, demonstrating the expressive power of Spanish.

Exercises on Placement of Adjectives

Exercise 1: Identify the Correct Order

Choose the sentence that correctly matches the description given.

A book that is interesting (an interesting book):

a) Un libro interesante

b) Interesante un libro

An old city (referring to age):

a) Una ciudad vieja

b) Vieja una ciudad

Beautiful flowers (emphasis on beauty):

a) Flores hermosas

b) Hermosas flores

Exercise 2: Rearrange the Sentences

Rearrange the words to form a correctly ordered Spanish sentence.

rojo / un / coche (a red car)

inteligentes / mujeres / Las (The intelligent women)

pequeño / gato / un (a small cat)

Answers

Exercise 1:

a) Un libro interesante - Correct because the adjective "interesante" follows the noun "libro," adhering to the standard post-nominal position in Spanish.

a) Una ciudad vieja - Correct as "vieja" comes after "ciudad," following the typical noun-adjective order in Spanish.

b) Hermosas flores - Correct because placing "hermosas" before "flores" emphasizes the beauty of the flowers, showcasing how adjective placement can convey subjective qualities or emphasis.

Exercise 2:

Un coche rojo - This order places the adjective "rojo" after the noun "coche," correctly forming the phrase for "a red car."

Las mujeres inteligentes - Here, "inteligentes" follows "mujeres," the correct structure for "The intelligent women."

Un gato pequeño - "Pequeño" is correctly placed after "gato" to describe "a small cat."

Descriptive Adjectives

Descriptive adjectives breathe life into nouns, painting them with characteristics of color, size, personality, and beyond. They transform a simple "car" into "a shiny red car," turning plain sentences into vivid stories.

Colors: Spanish colors act as adjectives, adapting to the nouns they describe. "Rojo" (red), "azul" (blue), "verde" (green), and "amarillo" (yellow) are just the beginning. To say "the green tree," you'd use "el árbol verde." Notice how the adjective follows the noun and doesn't change according to gender, though some color adjectives like "rojo" become "roja" if describing a feminine noun.

Size: Describing the size of objects or people involves adjectives such as "grande" (big), "pequeño" (small), "alto" (tall), and "corto" (short). These adjectives do change with the gender and number of the nouns they modify. For instance, "un perro grande" (a big dog) but "una casa grande" (a big house).

Personality: When describing personality traits or human qualities, Spanish offers a rich array of adjectives. "Amable" (kind), "valiente" (brave), "alegre" (happy), and "serio" (serious) allow you to sketch detailed portraits of people's characters. Remember, these adjectives must agree in gender and number with the person they describe, e.g., "un niño valiente" (a brave boy) and "una niña valiente" (a brave girl).

Using descriptive adjectives effectively means paying attention to the noun's gender and number and placing the adjective to best convey the intended meaning. Practice combining nouns with various descriptive adjectives to expand your vocabulary and express yourself more vividly in Spanish.

Exercises on Descriptive Adjectives

Exercise 1: Match the Adjective to the Correct Sentence

Choose the adjective that best completes each sentence.

El gato es muy ___ . (friendly)

a) amable

b) verde

c) alto

La camisa es ___ . (blue)

a) azul

b) grande

c) alegre

Ese libro es ___ . (interesting)

a) interesante

b) corto

c) pequeño

Exercise 2: Adjective Agreement

Choose the correct form of the adjective to agree with the noun.

Las flores son ___ . (beautiful)

a) hermoso

b) hermosa

c) hermosas

El edificio es ___ . (tall)

a) alto

b) alta

c) altos

Los niños son ___ . (happy)

a) alegre

b) alegres

c) alegres

Answers

Exercise 1:

a) amable - Correct because "amable" means friendly, fitting the description for a cat's demeanor.

a) azul - Correct as "azul" translates to blue, which is used to describe the color of a shirt.

a) interesante - Correct because "interesante" means interesting, suitable for describing a book.

Exercise 2:

c) hermosas - Correct because "hermosas" is the feminine plural form of "hermoso," agreeing with "las flores."

a) alto - Correct as "alto" is the masculine singular form of the adjective, agreeing with "el edificio."

b) alegres - Correct because "alegres" is the plural form, matching the plural noun "los niños" and conveying happiness.

Demonstrative Adjectives

Demonstrative adjectives are the pointing fingers of language, directing attention to specific nouns. In Spanish, these adjectives include "este" (this), "ese" (that), "aquel" (that over there), and their plural and feminine forms. They change to match the gender and number of the nouns they modify, providing a precise way to refer to objects and people in relation to space and distance.

- Este/Esta (This): "Este" for masculine and "esta" for feminine nouns refer to something close to the speaker. "Este libro" (this book) when holding a book, or "esta mesa" (this table) when sitting at a table.

- Ese/Esa (That): "Ese" for masculine and "esa" for feminine nouns are used for items that are relatively close but not immediately next to the speaker. "Ese coche" (that car) when pointing to a car across the street.

- Aquel/Aquella (That over there): "Aquel" for masculine and "aquella" for feminine nouns point to something further away in distance or time. "Aquel edificio" (that building over there) for a distant building.

The plural forms ("estos/estas," "esos/esas," "aquellos/aquellas") follow the same rules, allowing you to refer to multiple items. For example, "esos libros" (those books) or "aquellas casas" (those houses over there).

Exercises on Demonstrative Adjectives

Exercise 1: Choose the Correct Demonstrative Adjective

Select the correct demonstrative adjective to complete each sentence.

___ zapatos son muy cómodos. (These)

a) Este

b) Estos

c) Ese

___ ventana está abierta. (That)

a) Esta

b) Esa

c) Aquella

___ montañas son hermosas. (Those over there)

a) Estas

b) Esas

c) Aquellas

Exercise 2: Match to the Correct Gender and Number

Match the noun to the appropriate demonstrative adjective.

Libros (books)

Casa (house)

Árboles (trees)

a) Esta

b) Esos

c) Aquellos

Answers

Exercise 1:

b) Estos - Correct because "estos" is the plural masculine form of "este," used to refer to multiple items close to the speaker.

b) Esa - Correct as "esa" is the singular feminine form of "ese," used for a single item not immediately next to the speaker but still relatively close.

c) Aquellas - Correct because "aquellas" is the plural feminine form of "aquella," used for items that are far away from the speaker.

Exercise 2:

Libros - b) Esos (Esos libros) - "Esos" correctly matches the masculine plural noun "libros," referring to books that are not immediately close to the speaker.

Casa - a) Esta (Esta casa) - "Esta" is the singular feminine form, correctly matching "casa" and indicating proximity to the speaker.

Árboles - c) Aquellos (Aquellos árboles) - "Aquellos" is the masculine plural form, suitable for referring to "trees" that are far away.

Possessive Adjectives

Possessive adjectives in Spanish, much like their English counterparts, signify ownership or a relationship to something or someone. However, they add an extra layer of intricacy by changing form to agree with the gender and number of the nouns they modify. This aspect of Spanish possessive adjectives enriches the language, allowing speakers to convey possession more precisely.

Spanish has two sets of possessive adjectives: short-form and long-form, each serving a slightly different purpose and agreeing with the noun in gender and number.

Short-form Possessive Adjectives:

These are the most commonly used and include "mi" (my), "tu" (your), "su" (his, her, its, your formal), "nuestro" (our), and "vuestro" (your, plural in Spain). They precede the noun and must match it in number (and gender, for "nuestro" and "vuestro"). For example:

- "Mi libro" (My book) and "Mis libros" (My books)

- "Nuestra casa" (Our house) and "Nuestras casas" (Our houses)

Long-form Possessive Adjectives:

These are used for emphasis or clarity and appear after the noun, which is a unique feature compared to English. They include "mío" (mine), "tuyo" (yours), "suyo" (his, hers, yours formal), "nuestro" (ours), and "vuestro" (yours plural in Spain). They agree with the noun in gender and number, such as:

- "Libro mío" (Book of mine)

- "Casas nuestras" (Houses of ours)

Understanding the dual form of possessive adjectives in Spanish and their correct usage allows for more nuanced expression of ownership and relationships.

Exercises on Possessive Adjectives

Exercise 1: Choose the Correct Short-Form Possessive Adjective

Select the correct short-form possessive adjective to complete each sentence.

___ amigos van al cine. (Our)

a) Mi

b) Tu

c) Nuestros

He perdido ___ llaves. (My)

a) Mi

b) Tus

c) Sus

___ hermana es muy inteligente. (Your, singular informal)

a) Su

b) Tu

c) Nuestra

Exercise 2: Match the Noun to the Correct Long-Form Possessive Adjective

Match the noun to the appropriate long-form possessive adjective.

Perros (dogs)

Revista (magazine)

Zapatos (shoes)

a) Mías

b) Tuyos

c) Suya

Answers

Exercise 1:

c) Nuestros - Correct because "nuestros" is the masculine plural form of "nuestro," agreeing with "amigos" in gender and number, indicating ownership by "us."

a) Mi - Correct as "mi" does not change for gender and is singular, matching "llaves" in the sense that it is possessed by "me."

b) Tu - Correct because "tu" is the singular form indicating ownership by "you" (singular informal), matching "hermana" in the sense of possession.

Exercise 2:

Perros - b) Tuyos - "Tuyos" is the correct match because it is the masculine plural form, agreeing with "perros" in number and implying the dogs belong to "you."

Revista - c) Suya - "Suya" matches "revista" in being singular and feminine, indicating the magazine belongs to "him, her, you (formal)."

Zapatos - b) Tuyos - "Tuyos" is repeated here as the correct match for "zapatos," which are plural, indicating the shoes belong to "you."

Quantitative Adjectives

Quantitative adjectives provide essential information about the number or amount of nouns they describe, offering clues about quantity without specifying an exact number. In Spanish, these adjectives must agree in number with the nouns they modify, playing a crucial role in conveying "how much" or "how many."

Common quantitative adjectives include "mucho" (much, many), "poco" (little, few), "alguno" (some, any), and "ninguno" (none). Their usage highlights the amount or extent of something, significantly impacting the noun agreement in sentences.

- Mucho/Mucha/Muchos/Muchas: Expresses a large quantity or degree. It changes to match the gender and number of the noun. For example:

    o "Mucho dinero" (A lot of money) and "Muchas personas" (Many people)

- Poco/Poca/Pocos/Pocas: Indicates a small amount or degree. Adjusts according to the noun it modifies:

    o "Poca paciencia" (Little patience) and "Pocos libros" (Few books)

- Alguno/Alguna/Algunos/Algunas: Means "some" or "any," used to describe an indefinite quantity. It varies with the noun's gender and number:

    o "Algunos días" (Some days) and "Alguna idea" (Some idea)

- Ninguno/Ninguna: Signifies "none" or "not any," and like the others, agrees in gender and number with the noun, though it typically is used in the singular form due to its negative nature:

    o "Ninguna solución" (No solution)

Mastering quantitative adjectives involves understanding their agreement with nouns and their impact on the sentence's meaning.

Exercises on Quantitative Adjectives

Exercise 1: Choose the Correct Quantitative Adjective

Select the correct form of the quantitative adjective to complete each sentence.

___ amigos quieren venir. (Some)

a) Alguno

b) Algunos

c) Ninguno

No tengo ___ tiempo para leer. (Much)

a) Mucho

b) Mucha

c) Muchos

Ella tiene ___ paciencia con los niños. (Little)

a) Poca

b) Pocos

c) Poco

Exercise 2: Match to the Correct Gender and Number

Match the noun to the appropriate quantitative adjective.

Ideas (ideas)

Problema (problem)

Flores (flowers)

a) Ningunas

b) Pocos

c) Algunas

Answers

Exercise 1:

b) Algunos - Correct because "amigos" is masculine and plural, and "algunos" agrees in gender and number, meaning "some."

a) Mucho - Correct as "tiempo" is masculine and singular, and "mucho" is used to express a large quantity or degree of something uncountable.

a) Poca - Correct because "paciencia" is feminine and singular, and "poca" indicates a small amount, agreeing in gender.

Exercise 2:

Ideas - c) Algunas - "Algunas ideas" is correct because "ideas" is feminine and plural, and "algunas" matches this in gender and number, indicating "some."

Problema - b) Pocos - This is a trick question; "problema" is singular and masculine, so the correct match would be "poco problema" for "little problem." "Pocos" is incorrect as it is plural and "problema" is singular.

Flores - c) Algunas - "Algunas flores" is correct for "some flowers," where "flores" is feminine and plural, so "algunas" agrees in gender and number.

Adjectives for Comparison

When we compare objects, people, or situations in Spanish, adjectives transform into tools of measurement. The language offers clear guidelines for creating comparisons, letting us express who is taller, which book is more interesting, or what is the best dish on the menu. The magic of comparative and superlative forms lies in their ability to rank and rate our world.

Comparatives: Spanish uses "más" (more) and "menos" (less) for comparisons, followed by "que" (than). To say someone is "taller than," you would say "más alto que." For "less interesting than," it's "menos interesante que." An example sentence might be, "Ella es más alta que yo" (She is taller than me).

Equality: To express equality, Spanish uses "tan ... como" (as ... as) for adjectives. If two things are equally good, you'd say, "Es tan bueno como" (It's as good as). A common use might be, "Este libro es tan interesante como aquel" (This book is as interesting as that one).

Superlatives: To express the highest degree of quality, Spanish adds "el/la/los/las más" (the most) before an adjective. For the tallest person, you'd say "la persona más alta." If something is the least interesting, it would be "el menos interesante." An example could be, "Él es el estudiante más inteligente de la clase" (He is the smartest student in the class).

Exercises on Adjectives for Comparison

Exercise 1: Create Comparative Sentences

Use the given information to create sentences using comparative adjectives.

Maria / intelligent / Juan

This coffee / good / that coffee

My car / fast / your car

Exercise 2: Expressing Equality

Fill in the blanks to express equality between the two subjects.

Mi hermano es ___ alto ___ mi primo. (as, as)

Esta silla es ___ cómoda ___ aquella silla. (as, as)

El perro de Juan es __ grande __ el perro de Luis. (as, as)

Answers

Exercise 1:

"Maria es más inteligente que Juan." - This sentence correctly uses "más ... que" to compare Maria's intelligence to Juan's, indicating Maria is more intelligent.

"Este café es mejor que ese café." - Using "mejor que" (better than) correctly compares the quality of two coffees.

"Mi coche es más rápido que tu coche." - "Más rápido que" is used for comparing speed, indicating the speaker's car is faster than the listener's.

Exercise 2:

"Mi hermano es tan alto como mi primo." - "Tan ... como" expresses that the brother and cousin are equally tall.

"Esta silla es tan cómoda como aquella silla." - This sentence correctly uses "tan ... como" to indicate equal comfort between two chairs.

"El perro de Juan es tan grande como el perro de Luis." - Equality in size between Juan's and Luis's dogs is accurately expressed with "tan ... como."

Irregular Adjectives and Common Mistakes

Spanish, like any language, has its exceptions, and adjectives are no exception. Irregular adjectives can trip up learners, especially when their comparative and superlative forms don't follow the regular patterns. Words like "bueno" (good) become "mejor" (better) and "el mejor" (the best) in their comparative and superlative forms, not "más bueno" or "el más bueno."

A common mistake is trying to apply regular rules to these irregular forms. To avoid this, familiarize yourself with irregular adjectives and their unique forms. Practice using them in sentences, and soon, distinguishing between regular and irregular patterns will become second nature, enhancing your fluency and confidence in Spanish.

Exercises on Irregular Adjectives and Common Mistakes

Exercise 1: Choose the Correct Form

For each adjective, choose the correct comparative or superlative form.

Bueno (good)

a) Más bueno

b) Mejor

c) Buenísimo

Malo (bad)

a) Peor

b) Más malo

c) Malísimo

Grande (big)

a) Más grande

b) Mayor

c) Grandísimo

Exercise 2: Fill in the Blanks with Irregular Forms

Complete the sentences with the correct irregular comparative or superlative form of the adjectives.

De todos los estudiantes, Juan es el ___ (inteligente).

Este problema es ___ (malo) que el anterior.

Mi casa es la ___ (grande) de la cuadra.

Answers

Exercise 1:

b) Mejor - Correct because "mejor" is the irregular comparative form of "bueno," not "más bueno."

a) Peor - Correct as "peor" is the irregular comparative form of "malo," instead of "más malo."

b) Mayor - Correct for comparing age or importance, but note that "más grande" is also used for physical size. This question tests knowledge of context-specific uses.

Exercise 2:

"De todos los estudiantes, Juan es el mejor." - "Mejor" correctly identifies Juan as the most intelligent among the students.

"Este problema es peor que el anterior." - "Peor" is used to compare the badness of two problems, indicating this one is worse.

"Mi casa es la mayor de la cuadra." - "Mayor" is used for indicating the largest in terms of age or importance, but if referring to size, "la más grande" would be correct. This sentence could be context-dependent.

9

Tackling Tenses

Present Tense Basics

Diving into the heart of Spanish, the present tense is your first essential step. This tense is the backbone of daily conversation, capturing the now of actions, feelings, and states of being. It's where the journey of verb conjugations begins, opening doors to expressing everything from what you do to what you love.

Formation and Usage

The present tense in Spanish might seem daunting with its verb conjugations, but it follows a logical pattern that, once mastered, becomes second nature. Verbs are categorized into three families based on their infinitive endings: -ar, -er, and -ir. Each group has its own conjugation blueprint for the present tense, adjusting the verb to match the subject of the sentence.

To conjugate a regular verb in the present tense, you start by stripping away the infinitive ending (-ar, -er, -ir) to find the stem. Then, you add a new ending based on the subject (I, you, he/she, we, you all, they).

-AR Verbs

For -ar verbs, the endings are as follows:

- Yo (I): -o

- Tú (You, informal): -as

- Él/Ella/Usted (He/She/You, formal): -a

- Nosotros/Nosotras (We): -amos

- Vosotros/Vosotras (You all, informal in Spain): -áis

- Ellos/Ellas/Ustedes (They/You all, formal): -an

Example: Hablar (to speak)

- Yo hablo

- Tú hablas

- Él habla

- Nosotros hablamos

- Vosotros habláis

- Ellos hablan

-ER Verbs

-ER verbs switch gears slightly with these endings:

- Yo: -o

- Tú: -es

- Él/Ella/Usted: -e

- Nosotros/Nosotras: -emos

- Vosotros/Vosotras: -éis

- Ellos/Ellas/Ustedes: -en

Example: Comer (to eat)

- Yo como

- Tú comes

- Él come

- Nosotros comemos

- Vosotros coméis

- Ellos comen

-IR Verbs

Finally, -ir verbs share similarities with both -ar and -er verbs, but with their own twist:

- Yo: -o

- Tú: -es

- Él/Ella/Usted: -e

- Nosotros/Nosotras: -imos

- Vosotros/Vosotras: -ís

- Ellos/Ellas/Ustedes: -en

Example: Vivir (to live)

- Yo vivo

- Tú vives

- Él vive

- Nosotros vivimos

- Vosotros vivís

- Ellos viven

Practical Usage

The present tense isn't just for stating facts or actions happening right now; it's also used for habitual actions ("I go to school"), general truths ("The sun rises in the east"), and near-future intentions ("We leave tomorrow").

To truly grasp the present tense, integrate it into your daily practice. Describe your routine, share what you like or dislike, and talk about your hobbies using the present tense. For example, "Yo estudio español todos los días" (I study Spanish every day) or "Nosotros escuchamos música" (We listen to music).

Exercises on Present Tense Basics

Exercise 1: Conjugate the Verb

Conjugate the following -ar, -er, and -ir verbs in the present tense for the given subjects.

Estudiar (to study) - Yo

Beber (to drink) - Ellos

Escribir (to write) - Nosotros

Exercise 2: Fill in the Blanks

Complete the sentences with the correct form of the verb in parentheses in the present tense.

Yo __ (comer) una manzana.

Tú __ (vivir) en Madrid.

Ella __ (hablar) tres idiomas.

Answers

Exercise 1:

Estudiar - Yo estudio. - For -ar verbs, the first person singular ending is -o, making "estudio" the correct form for "yo."

Beber - Ellos beben. - For -er verbs, the third person plural ending is -en, making "beben" the correct form for "ellos."

Escribir - Nosotros escribimos. - For -ir verbs, the first person plural ending is -imos, making "escribimos" the correct form for "nosotros."

Exercise 2:

Yo como una manzana. - "Comer" is an -er verb, and "como" is the first person singular form.

Tú vives en Madrid. - "Vivir" is an -ir verb, and "vives" is the second person singular form.

Ella habla tres idiomas. - "Hablar" is an -ar verb, and "habla" is the third person singular form.

Present Progressive Tense

The present progressive tense in Spanish is like a snapshot, capturing the motion and momentum of actions as they happen. It zooms in on the here and now, painting a vivid picture of ongoing activities. If the present tense tells us what you generally do, the present progressive shows us what you are doing right at this moment.

Formation and Mechanics

The present progressive is formed with a two-part recipe: the verb "estar" (to be) in the present tense plus a gerund, which is akin to the "-ing" form in English. For -ar verbs, the gerund ends in "-ando" (hablar → hablando), and for -er and -ir verbs, it ends in "-iendo" (comer → comiendo, vivir → viviendo).

Here's how you conjugate "estar" in the present tense, followed by a gerund:

- Yo estoy (I am)

- Tú estás (You are)

- Él/Ella/Usted está (He/She/You formal is)

- Nosotros estamos (We are)

- Vosotros estáis (You all are, informal in Spain)

- Ellos/Ellas/Ustedes están (They/You all formal are)

Putting It into Action

Imagine you're describing someone running through the park. In Spanish, you'd say, "Él está corriendo en el parque" (He is running in the park). The action is happening right now, unfolding as you speak.

The present progressive tense is your go-to for expressing actions in motion, offering a dynamic way to share your experiences and observations in real-time.

Exercises on Present Progressive Tense

Exercise 1: Forming the Present Progressive

Conjugate the verbs in the present progressive tense.

Yo __ (leer) un libro.

Nosotros __ (escribir) un correo electrónico.

Ellas __ (jugar) al tenis.

Exercise 2: Choose the Correct Gerund Form

Select the correct gerund form to complete the sentence in the present progressive.

Tú estás __ (comer).

a) comiendo

b) comer

c) comido

Yo estoy __ (vivir) en España.

a) vivido

b) viviendo

c) vivo

Él está __ (hablar) por teléfono.

a) hablado

b) hablando

c) habla

Answers

Exercise 1:

Yo estoy leyendo un libro. - "Leyendo" is the gerund form of "leer," and "estoy" is the present tense form of "estar" for "yo," correctly forming the present progressive.

Nosotros estamos escribiendo un correo electrónico. - "Escribiendo" is the gerund for "escribir," used with "estamos" (the present tense of "estar" for "nosotros") to indicate an ongoing action.

Ellas están jugando al tenis. - "Jugando" is the gerund form of "jugar," and "están" is the present tense of "estar" for "ellas," correctly forming the present progressive.

Exercise 2:

a) comiendo - Correct because "comiendo" is the gerund form of "comer," fitting the present progressive structure with "estás."

b) viviendo - Correct as "viviendo" is the gerund form of "vivir," used with "estoy" to describe an ongoing action.

b) hablando - Correct because "hablando" is the gerund form of "hablar," used with "está" to indicate an action happening in real-time.

Preterite Tense

Step back into the past with the preterite tense, Spanish's gateway to recounting events that have started and finished. This tense is the storyteller of completed actions.

Breaking Down the Preterite

The preterite tense has specific conjugation patterns for -ar, -er, and -ir verbs, each with its unique set of endings. Unlike the present progressive, which focuses on the present moment, the preterite wraps actions up with a sense of completion.

For -ar verbs, the endings are:

- Yo: -é

- Tú: -aste

- Él/Ella/Usted: -ó

- Nosotros: -amos

- Vosotros: -asteis

- Ellos/Ellas/Ustedes: -aron

Example with "hablar" (to speak):

- Yo hablé

- Tú hablaste

- Él habló

- Nosotros hablamos

- Vosotros hablasteis

- Ellos hablaron

For -er and -ir verbs, the endings merge and go like this:

- Yo: -í

- Tú: -iste

- Él/Ella/Usted: -ió

- Nosotros: -imos

- Vosotros: -isteis

- Ellos/Ellas/Ustedes: -ieron

Example with "comer" (to eat) and "vivir" (to live):

- Yo comí / viví

- Tú comiste / viviste

- Él comió / vivió

- Nosotros comimos / vivimos

- Vosotros comisteis / vivisteis

- Ellos comieron / vivieron

Narrating the Past

The preterite is perfect for telling stories, reporting past events, and listing completed tasks. It's the tense you use for summarizing your day, recounting a vacation, or narrating a book's plot.

Common scenarios and example sentences:

- "Ayer, yo vi una película." (Yesterday, I saw a movie.)

- "La semana pasada, ellos viajaron a México." (Last week, they traveled to Mexico.)

- "Tú terminaste el proyecto a tiempo." (You finished the project on time.)

The preterite tense serves as a clear marker of past actions, allowing speakers to delineate events with precision.

Exercises on Preterite Tense

Exercise 1: Conjugate in the Preterite

Conjugate the following verbs in the preterite tense for the given subject.

Comprar (to buy) - Yo

Beber (to drink) - Tú

Abrir (to open) - Ellos

Exercise 2: Fill in the Blanks

Complete the sentences with the correct form of the verb in parentheses in the preterite tense.

Nosotros __ (estudiar) para el examen ayer.

Ella __ (vender) su coche la semana pasada.

Vosotros __ (escribir) una carta.

Answers

Exercise 1:

Compré - "Comprar" is an -ar verb, and for "yo" in the preterite, the ending is -é, making "compré" the correct form.

Bebiste - "Beber" is an -er verb, and for "tú" in the preterite, the ending is -iste, making "bebiste" the correct form.

Abrieron - "Abrir" is an -ir verb, and for "ellos" in the preterite, the ending is -ieron, making "abrieron" the correct form.

Exercise 2:

Nosotros estudiamos para el examen ayer. - "Estudiar" is an -ar verb, and "estudiamos" is the correct form for "nosotros" in the preterite.

Ella vendió su coche la semana pasada. - "Vender" is an -er verb, and "vendió" is the correct form for "ella" in the preterite.

Vosotros escribisteis una carta. - "Escribir" is an -ir verb, and "escribisteis" is the correct form for "vosotros" in the preterite.

Imperfect Tense

The imperfect tense in Spanish, or "el imperfecto," acts like a time machine, transporting us back to ongoing or habitual actions in the past. It's the storytelling tense, perfect for setting scenes, describing repeated past routines, or talking about what things were like "back in the day." Unlike the preterite, which pinpoints specific completed actions, the imperfect paints the background, providing a sense of continuity in past narratives.

Formation and Function

The conjugation patterns for the imperfect tense are mercifully straightforward, offering a breath of fresh air to Spanish learners. For -ar verbs, the endings are -aba, -abas, -aba, -ábamos, -abais, -aban. For both -er and -ir verbs, the endings unify under -ía, -ías, -ía, -íamos, -íais, -ían.

Examples:

- "Hablar" (to speak): Yo hablaba, tú hablabas, él hablaba, nosotros hablábamos, vosotros hablabais, ellos hablaban.

- "Comer" (to eat) and "Vivir" (to live) share endings: Yo comía/vivía, tú comías/vivías, él comía/vivía, nosotros comíamos/vivíamos, vosotros comíais/vivíais, ellos comían/vivían.

Imperfect vs. Preterite:

Understanding when to use the imperfect versus the preterite is crucial. The imperfect is used for:

- Describing people, places, and situations in the past: "La ciudad era tranquila" (The city was peaceful).

- Talking about habitual actions: "Siempre comíamos juntos"

111

(We always ate together).

- Expressing the time and age in the past: "Eran las siete de la noche" (It was seven o'clock at night).

Exercises on Imperfect Tense

Exercise 1: Conjugate in the Imperfect Tense

Conjugate the following verbs in the imperfect tense for the given subject.

Jugar (to play) - Nosotros

Leer (to read) - Ella

Escribir (to write) - Yo

Exercise 2: Choose the Correct Usage

For each scenario, choose whether the imperfect or preterite tense is more appropriate.

Describing the weather on a specific day of a trip.

a) Imperfect

b) Preterite

Talking about what you used to do on weekends.

a) Imperfect

b) Preterite

Narrating a story about a day you met a famous person.

a) Imperfect

b) Preterite

Answers

Exercise 1:

Jugábamos - "Jugar" is an -ar verb, and for "nosotros" in the imperfect, the ending is -ábamos, making "jugábamos" the correct form.

Leía - "Leer" is an -er verb, and for "ella" in the imperfect, the ending is -ía, making "leía" the correct form.

Escribía - "Escribir" is an -ir verb, and for "yo" in the imperfect, the ending is -ía, making "escribía" the correct form.

Exercise 2:

b) Preterite - Describing the weather on a specific day of a trip refers to a completed action or condition at a specific point in time, making the preterite more appropriate.

a) Imperfect - Talking about habitual actions in the past, like what one used to do on weekends, is a classic use of the imperfect tense.

b) Preterite - Narrating a specific event, such as the day you met a famous person, calls for the preterite tense to indicate a completed action within a defined timeframe.

Future Tense

The future tense in Spanish, or "el futuro," is like peering into a crystal ball, revealing actions that have yet to unfold. It's utilized to express what will happen or what one will do, carrying a sense of certainty or intention about the future.

Conjugation and Alternatives

Conjugating verbs in the future tense involves adding endings directly to the infinitive form, regardless of whether the verb ends in -ar, -er, or -ir. The endings are -é, -ás, -á, -emos, -éis, -án.

Examples:

- "Hablar": Yo hablaré, tú hablarás, él hablará, nosotros hablaremos, vosotros hablaréis, ellos hablarán.

- "Comer": Yo comeré, tú comerás, él comerá, nosotros comeremos, vosotros comeréis, ellos comerán.

- "Vivir": Yo viviré, tú vivirás, él vivirá, nosotros viviremos, vosotros viviréis, ellos vivirán.

An alternative to the simple future tense is the "ir a" + infinitive construction, which is akin to the English "going to" form. It's widely used in everyday conversation to talk about plans or intentions.

Example Sentences:

- "Mañana lloverá." (Tomorrow it will rain.)

- "Voy a estudiar español esta noche." (I am going to study Spanish tonight.)

Choosing Between Future Forms:

The simple future tense is often used for predictions or certain future events, while the "ir a" construction is more common for immediate plans or decisions made in the moment. The choice between them can add nuance to your speech, reflecting the degree of certainty or the timing of the action.

- "Algún día viajaré por el mundo." (Someday I will travel around the world.) – Simple future for long-term intentions.

- "Voy a reservar los billetes ahora." (I am going to book the tickets now.) – "Ir a" for immediate plans.

Mastering both the future tense and the "ir a" construction allows for a richer expression of future actions and intentions.

Exercises on Future Tense

Exercise 1: Conjugate in the Future Tense

Conjugate the following verbs in the future tense for the given subject.

Decidir (to decide) - Ella

Trabajar (to work) - Nosotros

Estudiar (to study) - Yo

Exercise 2: Choose the Correct Form

For each sentence, choose whether the simple future tense or the "ir a" construction is more appropriate.

___ (Nosotros - ganar) el campeonato el próximo año.

a) ganaremos

b) vamos a ganar

Mañana ___ (yo - hacer) una tarta para el cumpleaños de mi hermano.

a) haré

b) voy a hacer

En 2050, la gente ___ (vivir) en Marte.

a) vivirá

b) va a vivir

Answers

Exercise 1:

Decidirá - "Ella decidirá" uses the future tense ending -á, correct for "ella" with the verb "decidir."

Trabajaremos - "Nosotros trabajaremos" incorporates the future tense ending -emos, appropriate for "nosotros" with the verb "trabajar."

Estudiaré - "Yo estudiaré" applies the future tense ending -é, fitting for "yo" with the verb "estudiar."

Exercise 2:

b) vamos a ganar - The "ir a" construction is more appropriate here, indicating a plan or intention for the near future.

b) voy a hacer - Again, the "ir a" construction suits best, suggesting an immediate plan or decision made for the near future.

a) vivirá - The simple future tense is used for predictions or certain events expected to happen in the more distant future.

Conditional Tense

Imagine you're holding a magic wand that can weave possibilities into your conversations, sketching out what could happen or what you'd like to happen. This is the power of the conditional tense in Spanish. It lets you explore hypothetical worlds, make polite requests, or muse about potential actions, all with a dash of courtesy and speculation.

Conjugating the Conditional:

The conditional tense is a dream for learners because of its uniformity. You simply tack on the endings -ía, -ías, -ía, -íamos, -íais, -ían to the infinitive form of the verb. It doesn't matter if the verb ends in -ar, -er, or -ir; the pattern stays the same, making it wonderfully predictable.

- To talk: hablar → hablaría

- To eat: comer → comería

- To live: vivir → viviría

Usage Scenarios:

- Polite Requests: "¿Podrías cerrar la puerta, por favor?" (Could you close the door, please?) adds a layer of politeness that's softer than a direct command.

- Hypothetical Situations: "Si ganara la lotería, viajaría por el mundo" (If I won the lottery, I would travel the world) lets you dream big and share those dreams with others.

- Speculative Advice: "Deberías hablar con ella, te sentirías mejor" (You should talk to her, you would feel better) offers advice gently, without presumption.

Exercises on Conditional Tense

Exercise 1: Conjugate in the Conditional Tense

Conjugate the following verbs in the conditional tense for the given subject.

Salir (to go out) - Tú

Tener (to have) - Yo

Ser (to be) - Ellos

Exercise 2: Fill in the Blanks

Complete the sentences with the correct form of the verb in parentheses in the conditional tense.

Nosotros __ (comprar) una casa grande si tuviéramos el dinero.

Ella __ (decidir) irse temprano si estuviera cansada.

Vosotros __ (poder) ayudarme con esto?

Answers

Exercise 1:

Salirías - "Tú salirías" is the correct form in the conditional tense for "tú" with the verb "salir," meaning "you would go out."

Tendría - "Yo tendría" is the correct form in the conditional tense for "yo" with the verb "tener," meaning "I would have."

Serían - "Ellos serían" is the correct form in the conditional tense for "ellos" with the verb "ser," meaning "they would be."

Exercise 2:

Nosotros compraríamos una casa grande si tuviéramos el dinero. - "Compraríamos" is the conditional form of "comprar" for "nosotros," indicating a hypothetical situation.

Ella decidiría irse temprano si estuviera cansada. - "Decidiría" is the conditional form of "decidir" for "ella," suggesting a conditional action based on a hypothetical state.

Vosotros podríais ayudarme con esto? - "Podríais" is the conditional form of "poder" for "vosotros," used here as a polite request or inquiry.

Subjunctive Mood

Now, step into a realm where wishes, doubts, and hypotheticals dance together — welcome to the subjunctive mood. Unlike the indicative mood, which deals with reality and certainty, the subjunctive invites us to express what we wish, hope for, or doubt.

Forming the Subjunctive:

The subjunctive mood might seem like a maze, but there's a method to its madness. For -ar verbs, swap the -ar for -e endings, and for -er and -ir verbs, opt for -a endings. Here's the twist: the nosotros form respects the vowel of the verb's group, making it a bit easier to navigate.

- To speak (hablar): hable, hables, hable, hablemos, habléis, hablen

- To eat (comer): coma, comas, coma, comamos, comáis, coman

- To live (vivir): viva, vivas, viva, vivamos, viváis, vivan

Key Triggers:

- Wishes and Desires: "Quiero que tengas éxito" (I want you to succeed) sends good vibes someone's way.

- Doubts and Uncertainties: "Dudo que llueva mañana" (I doubt it will rain tomorrow) expresses skepticism.

- Impersonal Expressions: "Es importante que estudies" (It's important that you study) gives advice without direct command.

Diving into the conditional tense and subjunctive mood opens up new dimensions of Spanish, allowing for nuanced conversations filled with hopes, dreams, and polite propositions.

Exercises on Subjunctive Mood

Exercise 1: Choose the Correct Subjunctive Form

Select the correct form of the verb in the subjunctive mood.

Es necesario que nosotros __ (limpiar) la casa.

a) limpiamos

b) limpiemos

c) limpiar

Prefiero que tú ___ (salir) temprano.

a) sales

b) salgas

c) salir

Espero que ellos ___ (volver) pronto.

a) vuelven

b) vuelvan

c) volver

Exercise 2: Fill in the Blanks with Subjunctive

Complete the sentences using the subjunctive form of the verbs in parentheses.

Ojalá que ___ (ser) un buen día.

Es importante que tú ___ (estudiar) para el examen.

Deseo que ustedes ___ (tener) éxito en su proyecto.

Answers

Exercise 1:

b) limpiemos - "Es necesario que nosotros limpiemos la casa." The subjunctive is used because it's an impersonal expression that triggers the subjunctive mood, expressing a necessity.

b) salgas - "Prefiero que tú salgas temprano." The subjunctive is correctly used following a personal preference, indicating a desire for someone else's action.

b) vuelvan - "Espero que ellos vuelvan pronto." The subjunctive is used as it follows an expression of hope, fitting the mood's use for wishes.

Exercise 2:

sea - "Ojalá que sea un buen día." The subjunctive form "sea" from "ser" is used to express a hope for a good day.

estudies - "Es importante que tú estudies para el examen." The subjunctive "estudies" from "estudiar" is used following an impersonal expression that gives advice.

tengan - "Deseo que ustedes tengan éxito en su proyecto." The subjunctive "tengan" from "tener" is used as it follows a wish for success.

10

Pronouns

Personal Pronouns

In the colorful tapestry of Spanish grammar, personal pronouns are the threads that connect our words to the world, representing people within the weave of sentences. Spanish personal pronouns are as vibrant and varied as the language itself, each carrying its unique role in the sentence, from the subject doing the action to the object receiving it.

The Cast of Characters:

- Subject Pronouns: "Yo" (I), "tú" (you informal), "él/ella" (he/she), "usted" (you formal), "nosotros/nosotras" (we), "vosotros/vosotras" (you all, informal in Spain), "ellos/ellas" (they), and "ustedes" (you all, formal in Latin America and plural you in Spain). They're the stars of the sentence, performing the action.

- Object Pronouns: These take two forms—direct and indirect. Direct object pronouns (me, te, lo/la, nos, os, los/las) receive the action directly, while indirect object pronouns (me, te, le, nos, os, les) tell to whom or for whom the action is done.

- Reflexive Pronouns: (me, te, se, nos, os, se) are used when the subject and object are the same, indicating actions done to oneself, like "Yo me lavo" (I wash myself).

Understanding when and how to use these pronouns is pivotal. While English often relies on context to drop pronouns, Spanish uses them to emphasize or clarify who's involved in the action, though subject pronouns can be dropped due to the verb conjugations often making the subject clear.

Exercises on Personal Pronouns

Exercise 1: Identify the Pronoun Type

For each sentence, identify whether the bolded pronoun is a subject, direct object, indirect object, or reflexive pronoun.

Ella canta muy bien. (She sings very well.)

Marcos me llama todos los días. (Marcos calls me every day.)

Yo le di el libro. (I gave him/her the book.)

Nosotros nos preparamos para salir. (We are getting ready to go out.)

Exercise 2: Choose the Correct Pronoun

Select the appropriate pronoun to complete each sentence.

__ (Yo/Nosotros) tengo dos hermanos. (I have two brothers.)

¿__ (Te/Le) gustan los chocolates? (Do you like chocolates?)

Ana y Carlos __ (los/les) vieron en el cine. (Ana and Carlos saw them at the cinema.)

Answers

Exercise 1:

Subject - "Ella" is the subject pronoun performing the action of singing.

Direct object - "Me" is the direct object pronoun receiving the action of the call.

Indirect object - "Le" is the indirect object pronoun indicating to whom the book was given.

Reflexive - "Nos" is the reflexive pronoun indicating that the subject and object are the same (the action of getting ready is performed by the subjects on themselves).

Exercise 2:

Yo - "Yo tengo dos hermanos" correctly uses the subject pronoun "Yo" to indicate that the speaker is performing the action.

Te - "¿Te gustan los chocolates?" correctly uses the direct or indirect object pronoun "Te" to ask about the listener's preference.

Los - "Ana y Carlos los vieron en el cine" correctly uses the direct object pronoun "los" to refer to a plural masculine object or group of people that Ana and Carlos saw.

Demonstrative Pronouns

Demonstrative pronouns in Spanish are like pointing fingers, directing attention to specific nouns near or far in time or space. They morph to match the gender and number of the nouns they highlight, serving as stand-ins for those nouns in a sentence.

Pointing Near and Far:

- Este/esta (this), estos/estas (these) for objects close to the speaker.

- Ese/esa (that), esos/esas (those) for objects somewhat distant.

- Aquel/aquella (that over there), aquellos/aquellas (those over there) for objects far from both the speaker and listener.

Unlike demonstrative adjectives, which modify nouns, demonstrative pronouns replace them, taking on the noun's role in the sentence. To distinguish between the two, remember pronouns stand alone, whereas adjectives always accompany a noun.

Gender and Number Agreement:

Just like the nouns they replace, demonstrative pronouns must agree in gender (masculine/feminine) and number (singular/plural) with them. This agreement is crucial for clarity and coherence in Spanish communication.

- "¿Ves ese libro? Quiero ese." (Do you see that book? I want that one.)

- "Prefiero esta camisa a aquella." (I prefer this shirt to that one over there.)

Exercises on Demonstrative Pronouns

Exercise 1: Select the Correct Demonstrative Pronoun

Choose the appropriate demonstrative pronoun to replace the noun in parentheses.

Me gusta _____ (la camisa) que está en la vitrina. (this/that/that over there)

¿Recuerdas _____ (los días) cuando éramos niños? (these/those/those over there)

Prefiero _____ (el coche) que vimos ayer. (this/that/that over there)

Exercise 2: Match the Demonstrative Pronoun to the Context

Match the given context with the correct demonstrative pronoun.

A book on the table next to you. (este/ese/aquel)

A building across the street. (este/ese/aquel)

A memory from many years ago. (este/ese/aquel)

Answers

Exercise 1:

Me gusta esa - "Esa" is the correct demonstrative pronoun for "la camisa" (feminine, singular) when referring to something somewhat distant, like in a showcase.

¿Recuerdas esos? - "Esos" matches "los días" (masculine, plural) and refers to days in the past, which are metaphorically distant.

Prefiero ese - "Ese" is used for "el coche" (masculine, singular) when referring to something that was seen yesterday, not immediately close but not far away.

Exercise 2:

A book on the table next to you. - este - "Este" is used for objects close to the speaker.

A building across the street. - ese - "Ese" refers to objects that are somewhat distant, like something across the street.

A memory from many years ago. - aquel - "Aquel" is used for things that are far in time or space, making it suitable for distant memories.

Possessive Pronouns

Possessive pronouns in Spanish are like secret codes that unlock the doors to ownership and belonging. They tell us to whom something belongs, wrapping the concept of possession in a cloak of gender and number agreement, distinguishing themselves from possessive adjectives with the finesse of a seasoned linguist.

The Basics of Possession:

Possessive pronouns include "mío" (mine), "tuyo" (yours), "suyo" (his, hers, yours formal, theirs), "nuestro" (ours), and "vuestro" (yours, plural in Spain). Unlike possessive adjectives, which sit snugly before a noun to modify it, possessive pronouns stand alone, replacing the noun altogether and agreeing with it in gender and number.

- Singular and Plural: "El libro es mío" (The book is mine), "Los libros son míos" (The books are mine).

- Masculine and Feminine: "La casa es nuestra" (The house is ours), "Las casas son nuestras" (The houses are ours).

Possessive Pronouns vs. Adjectives:

While "mi libro" (my book) uses a possessive adjective to modify "libro," "el libro es mío" uses a possessive pronoun, replacing "libro" to state ownership. This distinction clarifies possession without repeating the noun, making conversations smoother and more concise.

Exercises on Possessive Pronouns

Exercise 1: Choose the Correct Possessive Pronoun

Select the correct possessive pronoun to complete each sentence, ensuring it agrees in gender and number with the noun it replaces.

¿Es este tu coche? No, el coche es _____. (mío/tuyo/suyo)

Creo que estas llaves son _____. (nuestras/vuestras/suyas)

La mochila que encontré no es _____; debe ser _____. (mía/tuya/suya)

Exercise 2: Convert to Use Possessive Pronoun

Rewrite the following sentences using a possessive pronoun instead of the possessive adjective and noun.

Mi casa es grande.

Sus libros son interesantes.

Vuestras sillas son cómodas.

Answers

Exercise 1:

No, el coche es mío. - "Mío" correctly replaces "tu coche" indicating ownership and agrees in gender and number (singular, masculine).

Creo que estas llaves son nuestras. - "Nuestras" matches "llaves" (plural, feminine) indicating collective ownership.

La mochila que encontré no es mía; debe ser tuya. - "Mía" and "tuya" correctly replace "mi mochila" and imply potential ownership, both agreeing in gender and number with "mochila" (singular, feminine).

Exercise 2:

Mi casa es grande. → La casa es mía.

Sus libros son interesantes. → Los libros son suyos.

Vuestras sillas son cómodas. → Las sillas son vuestras.

Pronoun Placement Principles

Navigating the placement of pronouns in Spanish sentences is akin to setting pieces on a chessboard. Each pronoun type—direct, indirect, and reflexive—has its strategic position, either before the verb or attached to infinitives, gerunds, and affirmative commands, creating a delicate balance that, when mastered, can elevate your Spanish prowess.

The Placement Playbook:

- Standard Placement: Generally, direct (me, te, lo/la, nos, os, los/las), indirect (me, te, le, nos, os, les), and reflexive pronouns (me, te, se, nos, os, se) precede conjugated verbs: "Te amo" (I love you), "Se lo di" (I gave it to him/her).

- Infinitives and Gerunds: When an infinitive (to do) or a gerund (doing) follows a conjugated verb, pronouns can attach to their ends: "Voy a hacerlo" (I am going to do it) or "Voy haciendo" (I am doing it).

- Affirmative Commands: In commands, pronouns also attach to the end: "Dámelo" (Give it to me).

Navigating Pitfalls:

- Clarity Is Key: Ensure pronoun placement doesn't obscure the sentence's meaning. If attaching a pronoun makes a verb form cumbersome or unclear, consider the standard placement.

- Accent Marks: Adding pronouns to infinitives, gerunds, or commands may require an accent mark to maintain the correct word stress: "cómpralo" (buy it).

- Negative Commands: Unlike affirmative commands, negative commands place pronouns before the verb: "No me lo des" (Don't give it to me).

Exercises on Pronoun Placement Principles

Exercise 1: Choose the Correct Pronoun Placement

Decide where the pronoun should be placed in the following sentences.

Quiero comprarlo / Lo quiero comprar. (it)

Está escribiéndola / La está escribiendo. (it, feminine)

No tocarlo / No lo toques. (it)

Exercise 2: Add the Pronoun to the Verb

Given a pronoun and a verb, place the pronoun correctly, either attaching it or placing it before the verb.

Mirar (it) - ellos

No abrir (it) - tú

Decir (it to me) - usted

Answers

Exercise 1:

Both "Quiero comprarlo" and "Lo quiero comprar" are correct. The pronoun "lo" can either be attached to the infinitive "comprar" or placed before the conjugated verb "quiero," depending on emphasis or stylistic preference.

Both "Está escribiéndola" and "La está escribiendo" are correct. The pronoun "la" can be attached to the gerund "escribiendo" or placed before the conjugated verb "está."

"No lo toques" is the correct placement for a negative command. The pronoun "lo" must precede the verb in negative commands.

Exercise 2:

Mirar (it) - ellos → Ellos lo miran (Standard Placement) or Ellos van a mirarlo (Attached to Infinitive)

No abrir (it) - tú → No lo abras (Standard Placement in Negative Command)

Decir (it to me) - usted → Usted me lo dice (Standard Placement) or Dígamelo (Attached in Affirmative Command)

Dialogue Creation to Apply Pronouns

Crafting dialogues in Spanish offers a golden opportunity to wield pronouns with precision and flair. By integrating personal, demonstrative, and possessive pronouns into your conversations, you'll not only enhance the natural flow of your dialogue but also deepen your connection with the language's intricate beauty. Here's a guide to artfully mixing these pronouns into dialogues, peppered with strategies to keep your conversations lively and engaging.

Step 1: Identifying Pronouns in Action

First, let's break down the pronoun types:

- Personal Pronouns: "yo" (I), "tú" (you), "él/ella" (he/she), used for actions and feelings.

- Demonstrative Pronouns: "este" (this), "ese" (that), "aquel" (that over there), used to point out specific things.

- Possessive Pronouns: "mío" (mine), "tuyo" (yours), indicating ownership.

Step 2: Dialogue Construction Basics

Beginning with Personal Pronouns:

Start by establishing your characters and their actions using personal pronouns. This sets the stage for who's doing what in the dialogue.

Incorporating Demonstrative Pronouns:

Next, weave in demonstrative pronouns to add detail. Which objects are characters interacting with? Are these objects near or far? Demonstrative pronouns will add color and context to your story.

Sprinkling in Possessive Pronouns:

Possessive pronouns bring a sense of belonging and relationship into your dialogue. Use them to express connections between characters and objects or ideas.

Step 3: Strategies for Natural Flow

- Mix and Match: Don't shy away from combining different pronoun types in sentences to mirror the dynamic nature of real-life conversations.

- Reflect Reality: Think about how conversations flow in everyday life and try to replicate this natural rhythm in your dialogues.

- Repetition is Okay: In natural speech, people often repeat pronouns for emphasis or clarity. Feel free to do the same.

Sample Dialogues

Dialogue 1: At a Café

Juan: "¿Ves esta taza? Es mía."

- (Juan: "Do you see this cup? It's mine.")

Maria: "Sí, y aquel libro, ¿es tuyo también?"

- (Maria: "Yes, and that book over there, is it yours too?")

Juan: "No, ese es de Carlos."

- (Juan: "No, that one is Carlos's.")

Dialogue 2: Planning a Trip

Luisa: "Nosotros queremos ir a la playa este fin de semana."

- (Luisa: "We want to go to the beach this weekend.")

Pedro: "¡Buena idea! ¿Y el hotel? ¿Ya reservasteis algo?"

- (Pedro: "Great idea! And the hotel? Have you guys booked something?")

Luisa: "Sí, encontré uno cerca de esa montaña que tú mencionaste."

- (Luisa: "Yes, I found one near that mountain you mentioned.")

Dialogue 3: A Misunderstanding

Ana: "Esa mochila, creí que era mía."

- (Ana: "That backpack, I thought it was mine.")

Roberto: "No, esta es la tuya, y esa es la mía."

- (Roberto: "No, this one is yours, and that one is mine.")

Ana: "¡Ah! Entonces, ¿dónde está el mío?"

- (Ana: "Ah! Then, where is mine?")

By following these steps and strategies, you'll craft dialogues that not only demonstrate your grasp of Spanish pronouns but also breathe life into your conversations, making them as vibrant and varied as the language itself.

11

Your Spanish Grammar Journey Continues

Embrace the Adventure

Your journey through Spanish grammar has equipped you with essential tools, but the landscape of language is vast and ever-changing. Each conversation is a new adventure, every book a treasure island, and every mistake a lesson learned. The key to continued growth lies in curiosity, practice, and perseverance.

Language learning is a marathon, not a sprint. Embrace the process with patience and joy. Celebrate your progress, however small it may seem. Every new word learned, every sentence correctly structured, and every fear overcome in striking up a conversation adds to your linguistic wealth.

Dive into Immersion

Surround yourself with Spanish as much as possible. Watch movies and listen to music in Spanish, letting the rhythm and emotion seep into your understanding. Join language exchange meetups or find conversation partners online. Immersion is a powerful catalyst for fluency, turning passive knowledge into active skill.

Keep a Journal

Document your journey in a Spanish journal. Write down new words, expressions, and grammar rules you learn. Reflect on your experiences in Spanish, however simple your sentences may be. This not only reinforces your learning but also tracks your progress over time.

Read, Read, Read

Start with children's books or graded readers and gradually progress to novels, newspapers, and blogs in Spanish. Reading expands your vocabulary, exposes you to different grammatical structures, and deepens your cultural understanding.

Be Fearless

Mistakes are inevitable and invaluable. Each error is a stepping stone to improvement. Speak, write, and practice without fear. The more you use Spanish in real-life contexts, the more natural it will become.

Explore Cultural Contexts

Language is a window into culture. Explore the customs, history, and traditions of Spanish-speaking countries. This cultural immersion adds depth to your language learning, making it more meaningful and engaging.

Set Goals

Define clear, achievable goals for your Spanish learning. Whether it's to hold a 5-minute conversation, watch a movie without subtitles, or travel to a Spanish-speaking country, goals give you direction and motivation.

Resources for Further Study

- Online Courses: Platforms like Coursera and EdX offer courses from universities on Spanish language and culture.

- Language Learning Websites: Sites like FluentU and Spanish-Dict provide interactive lessons, dictionaries, and resources tailored to learners.

- Spanish Language Meetups: Platforms like Meetup.com host language exchange groups where learners can practice speaking.

- YouTube Channels: Channels dedicated to Spanish learning offer free lessons on grammar, vocabulary, and pronunciation.

As your Spanish grammar journey continues, remember that each day brings you closer to fluency. The world of Spanish is vast and beautiful, filled with stories to hear, songs to sing, and people to meet. Let your love for the language drive you forward, and may your journey be as rewarding as the destinations you'll reach. ¡Buena suerte y sigue adelante! (Good luck and keep going!)

www.ingramcontent.com/pod-product-compliance
Lightning Source LLC
Chambersburg PA
CBHW031421120626

46545CB00006B/2219